The Willing Victim

The Willing Victim

A Parent's Guide to Drug Abuse

George Birdwood

Foreword by Sir John Wolfenden

Secker & Warburg · London

First published in England 1969 by
Martin Secker & Warburg Limited
14 Carlisle Street, Soho Square, London W1V 6NN

Reprinted 1969
SBN 436 04300   9

Printed in Great Britain by
Northumberland Press Limited
Gateshead

CONTENTS

Acknowledgments   vii

Foreword by Sir John Wolfenden   ix

Preface   xi

1   WHO GETS ADDICTED ?   1
    What parents can do   23

2   THE SOFT DRUGS   26
    Marihuana   27
    Amphetamines   44
    Other soft drugs   61
    What parents can do   66

3   THE HARD DRUGS   71
    Opium and its derivatives   73
    Cocaine   78
    Addiction to the hard drugs   81
    What parents can do   97

4   LSD AND OTHER HALLUCINOGENS   100
    What parents can do   115

5   COMMUNITY ADDICTIONS   119
    Sleeping tablets, sedatives and tranquillizers   122

Contents

    Alcoholism   130
    Smoking   135
    What parents can do   141

6   THE TEENAGE ADDICT—WHY?   145

7   WHAT HAS BEEN AND COULD BE DONE   169

    Appendixes

I   FIRST-AID IN CASES OF OVERDOSAGE   191

II   DRUGS AND THE POLICE—WHAT TO DO IF A TEENAGER IS INVOLVED   194

III   ADDICTS' SLANG   198

IV   TRADE NAMES AND BRIEF DESCRIPTIONS OF COMMONLY USED DRUGS, WHICH COULD BE ABUSED   203

ACKNOWLEDGMENTS

Among many sources, too numerous to list individually, the following are particularly acknowledged:

BOOKS

Narcotics, Nature's Dangerous Gifts, by Norman Taylor (Delta Books, New York, 1963)

Commonsense about Smoking, by Dr C. M. Fletcher and others (Penguin, 2nd edition, 1965)

Nightmare Drugs, by Donald Louria (Pocket Books, New York, 1966)

Hashish: its Chemistry and Pharmacology (CIBA Foundation, Churchill, London, 1965)

The Book of Grass, edited by George Andrews and Simon Vinkenoog (Grove Press, New York, 1967)

The Marihuana Papers, edited by David Solomon (Signet Books, New York, 1966)

The Drug Scene in Great Britain, by Dr Max Glatt and others (Edward Arnold, London, 1967)

The Willing Victim

Drugs and the Police, by Terence Jones (Butterworth, London, 1968)

Aspects of Drug Addiction, by Martin Silberman (Royal London Prisoners' Aid Society, London, 1967)

Childhood and Adolescence, by J. A. Hadfield (Penguin, London, 1962)

Drug Addiction, by David P. Ausubel (Random House, New York, 1958)

Drug Addiction in Youth, edited by E. Harms (Pergamon, Oxford, 1965)

ARTICLES by Drs Thomas H. Bewley, R. N. & I. C. Chopra, P. H. Connell, Vincent P. Dole, Nathan B. Eddy, Griffith Edwards, D. G. Gillespie, Max M. Glatt, H. Halbach, D. R. Hills, Harris Isbell, Marie E. Nyswander, David J. Pittman, R. A. Sandison, Maurice H. Seevers, and many others published in *British Journal of Addiction, British Medical Journal, The Lancet, The Practitioner, Comprehensive Psychiatry, Journal of the American Medical Association, Bulletin on Narcotics, American Journal of Psychiatry, Addictions*, and other journals, as well as many publications issued by agencies of the U.S. Public Health Service and by official sources in Britain.

PAPERS given at meetings of the American Psychiatric Association, the World Psychiatric Association and other bodies by: Drs H. Akimoto, M. Bleuler, Peter Blos snr., John Bowlby, Albert Bryt, Helene Deutsch, A. M. Freedman, Edward J. Hornick, Margaret Lowenfeld, William H. McGlothlin, Jules H. Masserman, Thomas F. A. Plaut, Calvin F. Settlage, and many others.

FOREWORD by SIR JOHN WOLFENDEN

Here is plain speaking. Dr Birdwood does not mince his words. When he thinks a drug is dangerous he says so. And he gives his reasons.

He is writing primarily for parents, and, particularly for parents of teenagers, As a parent himself and as a doctor he is, if anybody is, qualified to talk turkey. He is not speculating or meditating, or musing, in a generally 'objective' way, about drugs and the use made of them by teenagers. His purpose is much more practical and to the point. He knows what the dangers are, and he sets them out, clearly and (if the word may be allowed) clinically.

There is an attitude towards this whole problem which goes by the description 'permissive'. With this approach Dr Birdwood as, again, a parent and a doctor has no truck. Some of these drugs are dangerous, to the personality and stability of your children and his and mine. He can say this, from a parental and professional point of view, without being charged with panic, sensationalism or fuddy-duddy obscurantism. In the present atmosphere of permissiveness it is no bad thing that a clear and definite voice should be heard.

PREFACE

Drug abuse is hot news. Pop-stars and other teenage idols are frequently in the headlines for being in unlawful possession of marihuana. Sensational accounts of the weird effects of LSD appear in newspapers and magazines, while articles and cheap paperbacks recount lurid tales of heroin addiction. Despite all this publicity, few parents seem to know much about the drugs that young people take or the reasons why they take them. Perhaps this is because basic information on drug abuse is hard to come by. Few books give factual descriptions and none of those at present available was written specially for parents. I have tried to fill this gap.

My aim has been to bring the whole subject firmly down to earth by stripping drug abuse of its mystical aura. This aura more than anything else, it seems to me, makes drug-taking appear attractive to the young and confuses the adult world in its search for remedies. The mystique must be removed if drug abuse is to be considered and dealt with objectively. In the first five chapters I have therefore described the origins and actions of the drugs themselves in simple terms, and tried to show why it is that some teenagers become their willing victims. Most of the material in this, the major part of the book, is factual and generally accepted. But in the two final chapters I have ventured to speculate on possible reasons why drug-taking should have become so widespread among the young, and given a personal view of measures for curtailing serious addiction. Like all the material in the book, these chapters are based on a comprehensive study of drug abuse rather than personal experience of treating addicts.

No doubt some critics who disagree with my views will claim that 'fools rush in . . .', but they might reflect that the angels are as timid as ever. So far as I have been able to discover, no acknowledged expert on either side of the Atlantic has published a guide on drug abuse for parents. Yet there is every reason to believe that drug-taking has its roots deep in family life, and that parents are more immediately concerned about the problem than any other section of the community.

I have assumed throughout that the reader is a parent, like myself, who would not happily contemplate the prospect of his or her own child taking drugs. However, those who favour a more lenient view will find that legalisation of marihuana is discussed in some detail, and may be interested to know that letters in *The Times* protesting the safety of habit-forming drugs are no new phenomenon. My great-grandfather, Sir George

Birdwood, wrote in *The Times* in January 1882 that smoking opium was 'absolutely harmless . . . as harmless as inhaling the smoke of a peat fire or vapour of boiling water'. Nobody in the 1960s has gone as far as that!

Finally, I must gratefully acknowledge the (often unwitting) help of many people whose ideas have found their way into these pages. A detailed list appears on page vii, but here I would like particularly to thank Sir John Wolfenden for writing the Foreword, the publishers and Dr John Rowan Wilson, who made this book possible, Dr Stanley Gilder and Dr Stephen Lock who made many valuable suggestions, and Mr Michael Pringsheim for steering me through the complexities of the law.

1

Who gets addicted?

Drug abuse can take many forms. In the widest sense it ranges from habitual chain-smoking at one end of the scale to morphine and heroin addiction at the other. Between these two extremes are alcoholics, marihuana smokers, experimenters with LSD, and many thousands who regularly rely on tablets to make them sleep, to pep them up or calm them down. All are to some extent dependent on a 'drug'. All have acquired a habit which is more or less harmful.

Definitions of drug abuse are usually more precise than this and include distinctions between addiction, habituation and different forms of dependence. These will be considered later, but at this stage it may be more helpful to look at the problem as a whole. A useful way of doing so is to compare drug-taking with an infectious disease such as measles. Each can only spread from one person to another. The infectious agent—drug or measles virus—can do nothing by itself; it depends on carriers (drug pedlars) and existing cases for its spread through the community, and can infect only those with low resistance.

But there is an important difference between drug-taking and acute infection. The child who catches measles recovers rapidly and acquires immunity as a result of the attack. Susceptibility to drug abuse, on the other hand, is often a feature of an immature personality and not readily corrected. Though many teenagers take drugs for a while and then grow out of the habit, those that are truly susceptible become chronically infected, especially if their friends are persuasive and the drug they take is itself habit-forming. Far from increasing resistance, this sort of 'infection' makes the drug-taker more susceptible than ever. Instead of immunity, he all too easily acquires a habit he cannot break.

For this reason, drug abuse can be more accurately compared with a longstanding infection such as tuberculosis, from which spontaneous recovery is slow if it takes place at all. Once such conditions get a hold in the community, a hard core of chronically infected cases becomes established and many susceptible individuals are exposed to infection. This is what has happened with drug abuse in Britain during the past ten years. The facts speak for themselves.

Before 1960, the number of teenagers addicted to the 'hard' drug heroin could be counted on the fingers of one hand. Since then they have multiplied by about one hundred times and now make up something between a quarter and a third of the estimated 3–4,000 heroin addicts in the country. This total has risen from under 500 in the same period, and the average age of those addicted has fallen steadily: it is now in the mid-twenties. Each year as the numbers increase the proportion of young addicts in their teens and early twenties rises even more steeply. Some start taking drugs when they are only thirteen or fourteen years old.

The increase in 'soft' drug-taking has followed the same pattern. Until about ten years ago, most teenagers hardly knew of the existence of amphetamine tablets (pep pills) or marihuana. Now many thousands of bored youngsters take excessive quantities of amphetamines illicitly every weekend for 'kicks'. Marihuana smoking is becoming at least as widespread, and young people have recently begun to experiment with LSD and other drugs. The core of infection is well established in the community, especially in London and some other cities and towns. Those most susceptible to it are teenagers.

Why should drug abuse among young people in Britain have spread so rapidly? It is customary to put the blame on increased availability of drugs—prescribed too freely by doctors, sold illicitly by pedlars, and shared out by takers among their friends. No doubt the fact that habit-forming drugs have been fairly easy to obtain has played a large part in their widespread abuse, in the same way that an epidemic of measles is impossible without the appropriate virus. On the other hand, an epidemic of any kind can spread only when large numbers of people have low resistance to infection. At this point it is easy to get into an updated version of the old argument about the chicken and the egg: which came first, the drug or the susceptible teenager? The fact is that both are essential ingredients of drug abuse. As we shall see in a later chapter, there are numerous reasons why many more teenagers should be susceptible than in the past, and to a large extent the greater availability of drugs is a response to increased demand. Unfortunately, official approaches to the problem have largely ignored this aspect of it. The susceptible teenager has been almost completely left out of account.

Official action to curb drug abuse has concentrated instead on control of supplies and treatment of established addicts. Even here, successive governments have tended to drag their feet; belated and weak half-measures were introduced only when it became obvious that the problem would not quietly go away by itself. Unauthorized possession of certain hard and soft drugs has now been illegal for several years, but there is little evidence that the thousands of convictions for this offence have made it more difficult to obtain black-market supplies. It is to be hoped that the restrictions on prescribing hard drugs—introduced in spring 1968—will prove more successful. Though treatment centres for hard-drug addicts were set up at the same time, they are being run on a shoestring and have no compulsory powers. It is doubtful whether they can effect many cures. Soft drug-takers are even worse off; in most areas there are no special treatment facilities for them at all. Some controls have been placed on the closing time of the sort of clubs where drugs commonly circulate, the police have been given wider powers of search, and several forces have set up special drug squads. Traffic in habit-forming drugs seems to be flourishing just the same.

Viewed as a public health operation to control the spread of an infectious disease and treat its victims, these official measures have so far been a dismal failure. The number of new cases of drug abuse continues to rise and the prospects of cure are little if any higher than they would be without treatment. Worst of all, apart from a half-hearted attempt to disseminate information about drugs in schools, nothing special has been done to protect teenagers. Conspicuously absent from recent legislation, for instance, has been any recognition that young people are particularly at risk. The law makes no distinction between offering heroin to a man of fifty or a girl of fifteen. This is in sharp contrast to the United States, where the drug problem is admittedly much more serious. There an adult convicted of selling heroin to a person under eighteen receives a sentence of between ten years and life (which means life, without parole or remission) for a first offence. For a subsequent offence, even the death penalty can be invoked. By contrast, the much more lenient sentences prescribed in Britain are insufficient to deter pedlars and addicts from introducing youngsters to a drug habit.

All this is cold comfort for parents. It means that official action has in all probability failed to reduce the chances of a susceptible teenager being offered habit-forming drugs. Of course, even adequate control measures could not be expected to solve the problem by themselves. What is needed in addiction is the sort of broad public health approach which has gradually overcome the great epidemic infectious diseases—cholera, smallpox, tuberculosis, diphtheria, typhoid, poliomyelitis. Though some have been defeated by immunization or modern drugs, a good deal of the credit must go to more general measures for keeping infection at bay and improving resistance to it. Our towns are safer to live in today than in the past because most people eat a well-balanced diet, understand something about hygiene, and live in better houses with clean water, proper drainage and regular refuse disposal. In other words, the emphasis has been as much on healthy people and the conditions in which they live as on disease.

A comparable approach to the problem of drug abuse among young people is urgently required. In addition to control of supplies and reducing the pool of infection by treating or isolating existing cases, teenagers must be 'vaccinated' against the spreading epidemic of drug abuse. Suitable measures might include better upbringing in childhood, more opportunities for children and adolescents to find outlets for their energies and abilities, and adequate instruction about drugs in schools. Much more attention should also be paid to the susceptible teenager and the sort of company in which he may be exposed to 'infection'. Parents and teachers need to know all about drug-taking and be able to spot its earliest signs. And there must be proper facilities for effective treatment, so that diagnosis can be followed by a reasonable prospect of cure.

Few of these things can be accomplished by the

hotch-potch of ministries, voluntary organizations, churches, welfare services, police officers, psychiatrists, doctors, probation officers and many others who struggle with the problem at present. Until a broad public health approach is adopted, they will continue to fight a losing battle. Drug abuse is essentially a social problem with its roots in the nature of society as a whole, and in the family life of its victims in particular. It will be solved not by medical or legal measures alone but by concerted action. This is where parents come in. There are two main fields in which they can act; first within their own family and, second, by pressing for the necessary changes in social policy. The purpose of this book is to help them do both these things by providing basic information on drugs and drug-takers.

The first thing that many parents will want to know is how to tell whether their own children are at risk. Obviously this will depend partly on susceptibility and partly on the company they keep. Unfortunately the concept of susceptibility is still too vague for precise definition. Nobody can yet identify an addiction-prone teenager with any certainty before he turns to drugs. Because drug-takers are of many types and comparatively few suffer from other mental disorders, psychiatrists have difficulty in recognizing them as other than immature personalities. But this does not mean that prevention is impossible. Well-informed, observant parents who know the weaknesses of their own children are likely to feel almost instinctively when they are at risk.

Where does susceptibility begin? If everybody could

follow Shaw's cynical advice, 'take the utmost care to get well born and well brought up', there would be a great deal less drug abuse, for there is good reason to believe that susceptible individuals are both born and made. Little is yet known about the role of inheritance—and in any event nothing can be done about it —but there is abundant evidence that the best way to make an addict is to bring him up badly. A later chapter will therefore be devoted to some of the changes in upbringing and adolescence which seem to have been partly responsible for the recent increase in drug-taking. No account of addiction could be complete without some discussion of this difficult subject.

Unfortunately, the very nature of the problem means that many of the parents most in need of advice are the least likely to receive it. Addicts' families show a consistently high rate of matrimonial difficulties, broken homes, delinquency, criminality and alcoholism. Such a home is probably the most frequent breeding-ground for the addiction-prone or delinquent teenager. On average he is not unintelligent, but he may have psychological difficulties, lack standards of behaviour, and find it hard to make friends, hold down a job or cope with life in general. With little sense of security, mistrusting society and yet seeking companionship, he is wide open to the spurious attractions offered by a criminal or drug-taking clique. For want of an adequate father, the susceptible adolescent has often been over-dependent on his mother during childhood. When he reaches his teens he resents this, because it makes him feel a child, and he breaks away to show his independence. But independence is precisely what he lacks. Dependence on mother is soon replaced by dependence on dubious friends or habit-forming drugs. Since divided, inadequate or irresponsible parents lie at the very root of this problem, advice to them on drugs, delinquency or any other topic is likely to be of little avail. Here, society will probably have to take a larger hand than at present. Some prevention may be possible if a way can somehow be found to provide what is really lacking—a stable upbringing in a stable home. Organizations concerned about the welfare of young people might play a useful part in stimulating thought and action in this field.

However, many addiction-prone teenagers come from divided but by no means delinquent families, and others from what seem—to the parents at any rate—to be normal, happy homes. Indeed, one of the most worrying aspects of the recent spread of drug-taking in Britain is the involvement of so many outwardly normal young people. The illusion that all is well may be abruptly shattered for their parents by smelling the unmistakable bonfire aroma of marihuana smoke or finding a discarded heroin syringe. Casting round for explanations, the distressed parents ask themselves where they 'went wrong'—and find few clear answers. As we shall see later, a whole series of minor influences—apparently trivial in themselves—can conspire together during childhood and adolescence to produce a susceptible teenager. In some cases warning signs were present but neglected because they seemed unrelated to drug problems. The teenager may always have been 'difficult', wilful, or easily led as a

9

child; he may even have required psychiatric help. More probably he will just have been rather immature for his age, possibly with the result that he (or she) seemed a particularly amenable and well-behaved child. Nobody realized that he might be addiction-prone because the concept was never mentioned. Of course, resistance to 'infection' varies, and occasionally falls to a low ebb even in relatively stable individuals. A familiar parallel is the young man 'caught on the rebound' by a totally unsuitable girl.

Though susceptibility varies from time to time and person to person, there is probably no such thing as complete resistance to an offer of drugs. Nobody inherits an ideal personality or has a perfect upbringing. Everyone makes mistaken decisions or bad friends at one time or another—particularly during the turbulent years of normal adolescence. The chance to try drugs may coincide with a brief period of boredom or loneliness, or of heightened susceptibility after an emotional family row, failing (or passing!) an exam, or being jilted by a girl friend. The chance may be taken not because upbringing was at fault in some major respect, but because a number of relatively minor circumstances happened to coincide.

An example may help to make the matter clear. Doctors and nurses might reasonably be thought less addiction-prone than average, yet statistics have shown higher rates for them than other occupational groups. Knowing the risks and having a reasonably stable personality are not enough. Under sufficient emotional stress almost everyone can become addiction-prone. Parents need to be on the look-out for such circumstances. Forearmed with a basic knowledge of drug-taking, they have a better chance than any outsider of spotting when their own children are likely to run the risk of experimenting with habit-forming drugs.

It might be said that the doctor who becomes an addict has—however inadequately—diagnosed his own illness. He senses a need in himself for treatment with a particular drug whose effects and dangers are well known to him. For a while the drug enables him to escape from his difficulties; it fills a need. The same can be said of all susceptible individuals, though the need is seldom apparent as such. It is more likely to express itself as boredom, delinquency, frustration, a desire for 'kicks'. Even if the individual himself perceives a need for help there is often nowhere to turn. For many susceptible teenagers the chance of taking habit-forming drugs is in fact the only chance of 'treatment' that they get. Yet there are very real objections to treating a vaguely-felt desire to escape from life's troubles by taking potent substances in ignorance of their dosage or effects. Such uncontrolled self-medication easily leads to persistent overdosage, until the drug begins to master the taker.

It is generally speaking true of all addictive drugs that their action is short-lived and more or less pleasant. They may be stimulating, calming, or hallucination-producing, but more important is the euphoria or sense of enjoyment which accompanies the other changes and brings the taker back for more. Those habit-forming drugs that have a place in medicine at all are used to relieve pain or alter mood for a few hours at most. None permanently cures any disease.

None is well suited to long-term treatment. All are in some degree addictive. With prolonged use their ill-effects gradually take over from any initial benefits. Physical and mental health are undermined, work is adversely affected or becomes impossible, family and social life are disrupted and others are introduced to the habit. Such are the dangers of the uncontrolled self-medication known as drug abuse.

Seeking only immediate relief or pleasure, if the drug-taker no longer achieves his aim with a particular dose, he increases it. In his childlike search for immediate gratification he is unaware of—or does not want to acknowledge—the future. Mention of it is often confined to such idealistic goals as a personal search for truth or banning nuclear weapons, not tomorrow's food and shelter or next year's job. Such a person is less well suited than other members of the community to choose what is best for him in practical terms; and quite unsuited to selection and control of his own 'treatment'. Yet there may be nowhere else to turn. He may have left home and be separated physically from his parents, or feel that they are the main cause of his troubles anyway. Unable to find a niche in life, unclassified as yet by the psychiatrists, the susceptible teenager must often seek his own salvation.

Here again, parents' organizations might be able to help. First, there seems to be a real place for some kind of youth advisory service, to which young people in difficulties of any sort could go directly for assistance. Second, it might be worth looking into the possibility of preventive schemes designed to spot teenagers most at risk—alone in large towns, for instance—so as to take action before rather than after they have turned to drugs or crime. In such matters individual parents can do little, but organized groups could probably exercise sufficient influence to get things done.

Despite all that has been said and written about drug abuse in recent years, the concept of the susceptible teenager has received little attention. Public discussion has usually centred instead on much more newsworthy topics—established addicts and the drugs they take. Consequently a sort of mystique has been allowed to build up in which the drug-taker is a colourful figure risking death for the sake of his drug. Pop-stars, the folk-heroes of our time, frequently get their pictures on the front page and their names into the headlines for being in illegal possession of marihuana or amphetamine. On one hand, this kind of publicity has the effect of a well-conducted advertising campaign; people who had never heard of the product begin to wonder whether to try it. On the other hand, there is the attraction of the unknown, the illegal, the dangerous—of risking all for the chance of entering another, more exciting world. Moreover, 'everybody smokes cigarettes, and they're dangerous. Why shouldn't I try marihuana?' More by accident than design, the already susceptible individual—the first stage on the road towards addiction—is softened up by publicity for the second stage: the offer of addictive drugs.

Describing the essential ingredients of addiction as a susceptible individual and a habit-forming drug is like saying that football consists of the player and the ball. It ignores the rest of the team, the opposing side and the spectators. It ignores, too, the fact that there is a game to be learned. A person who had never heard of football would hardly know how to begin if he found himself suddenly put down in the middle of a pitch, alone with the ball. This is quite simply not the way the game is played. True, the lone footballer might kick the ball around for a while, but when he had stubbed his toes a few times and become bored for want of other players the game would cease, probably for good. Much the same applies to drug abuse. It is, especially in its early stages, a social pursuit. The lone novice might take an experimental dose, but since the initial effects of a drug are often unpleasant, the first dose would probably also be the last. Clearly, something more is needed. For the individual, the game begins with recruitment, with the persuasive *offer* of habit-forming drugs.

This offer is by no means always made by criminal drug-pedlars. Indeed, in Britain they are still a comparatively rare breed, yet drug abuse flourishes as never before. Why is this? Again, sport can provide a useful parallel. Since football is generally held to be a 'good thing', players have the active support of parents, schoolteachers, youth club leaders, team managers and other responsible people in recruiting young members. Tragically, drug-takers also obtain a good deal of more or less unintentional support from what are usually thought of as responsible institutions and individuals. Their role is not confined to permissive acceptance, or even to the kind of cheap publicity about drug-taking that helps sell newspapers and build up viewing figures. It extends even to the initial offer itself.

14

Widespread advertisement of tobacco and alcohol by respected commercial concerns is accepted as the social norm. Huge profits are made, governments join in by reaping handsome tax rewards, and gestures of dissent from those concerned for the public health are lightly swept aside. It is the 'done thing' to smoke, to have one for the road. The risks tend to be ignored, since life is dull and needs a little excitement now and again to give it spice; smoke, drink and be somewhat less bored, for tomorrow we die. Society's opprobrium is reserved for that virtuous, antisocial, non-conforming creature—the teetotal non-smoker. Respectable institutions and individuals aid and abet one another in introducing novices to habit-forming 'drugs'.

In some ways the role of the medical profession is even more questionable. Commerce may be persuasive, but at least it deceives neither its customers nor itself about the motive—profit. Doctors, on the other hand, belong to a learned profession expected to maintain impeccable ethical standards. Yet the awkward fact cannot be evaded that many susceptible individuals receive their first offer of habit-forming drugs from a medical practitioner. However good the intentions, an offer made in such circumstances is all the more dangerous; it is most unlikely to be refused. When anxious and therefore susceptible people who claim to be unable to sleep are given sleeping tablets, a temporary need all too often becomes a permanent problem. The same is true of the huge quantity of sedatives and tranquillizers prescribed for daytime worries. The short-term benefits are often very real, the long-term results of continuous therapy more dubious. Since barbiturates and other sedatives tend to lose their effect with time, the patient may then be no better than before starting treatment—which he dare not stop for fear of getting worse. In some cases the dose stays fairly steady, but in others it is slowly increased and the patient becomes quite seriously addicted. A later chapter is devoted to barbiturate abuse, but it is worth stressing here that patients who 'need' these drugs for more than purely short-term use do so because they have difficulty in coping with life, and are therefore liable to become dependent on them.

Much the same applies when 'pep' pills—stimulants of amphetamine type—are prescribed for depression or to reduce the appetite of overweight patients. They too are apt to become dependent, since they often lack the will-power to stop treatment. After some months the drug has little further value and is continued partly for its pleasant effects, partly to avoid the depression that follows withdrawal. Though doctors are becoming increasingly aware of these problems, many potentially habit-forming drugs are still being prescribed in excessive quantities.

More serious than this was the indirect part played by a very few doctors in introducing young people to hard drugs. Fortunately the prescribing ban which became effective in the spring of 1968 has now put a stop to the practice, but until then many addicts obtained grossly excessive supplies of heroin and cocaine on prescription. They then had sufficient to spare after satisfying their own needs to introduce novices to the habit. Though some of these doctors have since been convicted of various offences, others are apparently turning to the prescribing of addictive drugs not yet covered by the ban.

The classic criminal offer is relatively rare in Britain. In this, the 'pusher' or pedlar approaches a new recruit with an offer of free supplies of a powerful drug like heroin, which are maintained only until a habit is established. A high price is then put on the drug and the new addict has to find fresh novices, to whom he in his turn can sell supplies and thus earn enough to pay for his own. The snowball effect of this in spreading addiction is only too obvious. The recent rapid increase of heroin, amphetamine and marihuana abuse in this country seems to have been mainly by less pernicious methods—straightforward black-market peddling of stolen or illegally-imported drugs, and 'normal' social contact between drug-takers and others. For many established takers the introduction of new recruits is an essential part of the game. Without a constant flow of new players, the addiction 'game' would eventually cease. The offer may not be made with criminal intent but its success is a crucial factor in the survival of the drug-taker's way of life.

Persuasion to take drugs can take many forms. The newcomer may be told that they will make him less inhibited—'turn on, man, you'll really feel great', 'you'll never know the feeling till you try it for yourself'. He may need to be reassured that drugs are harmless—'you don't want to believe all those tales about drugs being dangerous, they're just cooked up by old fuddy-duddies to frighten you off', 'of course there's no danger', 'it's not habit-forming'. 'I can kick the habit [stop taking drugs] any time I want'. Sometimes blackmail is necessary—'don't be a spoilsport—join the party', 'he's frightened to try it', 'mummy said he shouldn't'.

Whether the offer is accepted depends on social attitudes and pressures as much as on the innate susceptibility of the individual. Human beings have a natural tendency to infect others with their enthusiasms and practices, and the susceptible teenager is attracted by the prospect of being admitted to membership of a charmed circle in which he can find friendship and escape the harsh realities of life. For the teenager or immature adult, there may be the additional attraction of doing something bad, forbidden or even dangerous. Everyone knows how much more exciting it is to pinch apples from an orchard, smoke at school, or go joy-riding in someone else's car than to do the same things legally. Finally, an offer of drugs may be accepted out of bravado, curiosity or simply because the new recruit is afraid of appearing 'chicken'.

When an offer of addictive material has sufficient appeal to be accepted by a large proportion of the population, what is sometimes called community addiction arises. Susceptibility is then determined as much by social conditions as individual character. The drug used satisfies a widespread need. In the past, opium-smoking in China was partly a response to grinding poverty and harsh conditions; marihuana and coca leaves are still used by poor people in a number of countries today to make life more tolerable. It is perhaps not too much to argue that the same principle applies to community addiction in supposedly civilized countries. Are not cigarette-smoking, drinking and over-indulgence in tablets a response to the harsh and hectic modern environment? People 'need' something to help them forget their cares.

Since community addictions become accepted as the social norm, they are tolerated and fostered without, in general, much thought being given to their desirability. Tobacco, alcoholic drinks, dependence on sleeping tablets may be innocuous or ruinous—it makes little difference. They are accepted just the same. Living in such a society, we should not be too surprised if drug pedlars and addicts become active in a less conventional and less desirable branch of the same trade.

Once an offer of drugs has been accepted and a taste acquired, they may be used intermittently or regularly. If a habit becomes established, the game begins in earnest, the form it takes depending on the drug used and the social setting. The novice generally starts with one of the soft drugs, but in the company of other devotees he is likely sooner or later to be offered stronger ones. For a few this is the start of a slippery slope ending with heroin, cocaine—and even death.

In the following chapters each of the habit-forming drugs likely to be encountered in this country will be considered in turn. Each has its own ritual game, just as customs have built up around the use of alcoholic drinks and smoking. Everyone knows that brandy and cigars tend to go together after dinner; the mere mention of the words conjures up an affluent scene, prosperous businessmen, Bentleys and Jaguars at the door. Equally, not much imagination is required to diagnose a public-bar regular's habits as 'roll-me-own and half a bitter'. The accumulated subconscious experience known as instinct enables us to recognize established community addictions at a glance—and with considerable accuracy of detail. Recognition of drug takers is less easy and certainly less precise; the rules of the game are less rigid. But associations like that between hippies, flower people and marihuana are unmistakable. Parents and teenagers should have little difficulty in spotting at least the groups and individuals likely to be abusing drugs.

Underlying all drug abuse is the fundamental *dependence** of the addict on his drug. If this dependence is purely *psychological*, the drug producing it is commonly described as 'soft'. The user may be convinced that he cannot do without its mental effects—or at least be very reluctant to do so—though in fact soft drugs can almost always be stopped abruptly. Marihuana and amphetamine are those most commonly used in England at present; stopping them may be unpleasant but it is not dangerous. In *physical dependence*, by contrast, some of the body's essential chemical processes become so accustomed to the presence of the drug that they cannot function properly without it. The 'hard' drugs, morphine and heroin, are the classical examples. During treatment they have to be withdrawn slowly to allow time for the body chemistry to return to normal. Sudden withdrawal deprives the body of a substance on which it has come to depend, and the *abstinence* or *withdrawal syndrome* results. This has both physical

* No attempt has been made in defining these terms to follow the World Health Organization's classification of drug dependence, which may be scientifically desirable but has little relevance for the general reader.

and mental features, since physical dependence is always accompanied by psychological dependence. Only the latter can be present by itself.

Drugs producing dependence of either type are often referred to as *habit-forming* or *addictive*, and the habit may be perpetuated in a number of ways. In general, the reasons for starting a drug are quite different from those for continuing to take it. Thus chain-smokers and alcoholics start smoking or drinking because they want to feel grown-up. Only later does craving develop, making the habit hard to break. Similarly, marihuana smokers try their first reefer for the sort of reasons already discussed, but they continue the practice because they enjoy the sense of escaping into the unreal world created by the effects of the drug. As much as for any other reason, established addicts on the hard drugs take the next dose because they feel so terrible when the effects of the previous one begin to wear off. Being physically as well as mentally dependent, they actually 'need' the next dose more than other drug users. This is one hallmark of true *addiction*. In the words of the dictionary definition, the addict has 'given himself up to the habit'.

But of course there is more to addiction than the establishment of a habit, however bad. Over a period of time, *habituation* takes place; the effects produced by a particular dose decline. The addict is said to have developed *tolerance*, and he needs ever-larger doses to produce the desired effect, or even to feel normal. Alternatively, he may abandon a particular drug and turn to stronger ones—the process known as *progression*.

Increasing use of soft drugs by young people, coupled

21

with the danger of progression to hard ones, are among the main reasons for public disquiet about drug-taking in Britain. But disquiet by itself can accomplish nothing; the scope for official action is limited and its results have frequently been disappointing. Where governments fail or fear to tread, parents may have more opportunities for useful intervention. They can also exert pressure that should help to overcome the traditional inertia of public bodies when action is required. Each section of this book will therefore conclude with a summary of suggestions for action which parents might usefully undertake, both within their own families and in a wider context. Since this chapter has been mainly concerned with the events leading up to drug abuse, the first summary deals with prevention. Proverbially, this should be better than treatment and will almost certainly prove so, since the results of treating established drug-takers are poor and more effective treatment would be very expensive. Unfortunately, a good deal of ignorance still surrounds the whole subject. We simply do not know, for instance, what happens to a susceptible teenager who does *not* take drugs, and can only assume he would be better off. Any advice given here or elsewhere at the present time could well fall victim to future research.

It is emphatically not the object of this book to frighten or excite the reader—except perhaps to action. If he or she feels while reading the following pages that the world is a black and evil place peopled with drug-takers, it may be profitable to reflect that the risk of any one person becoming seriously addicted is very small indeed. Most young people have enough good sense to refuse an offer of drugs; those who are susceptible seldom seek them and many never receive an offer. Even if they do, vigilant parents have a good chance of spotting trouble early enough to nip it in the bud before a habit is established.

When Freya Stark wrote 'happiness is the health of the spirit; nor is anything else to be counted a disaster except the perversion of the soul', she was not describing drug addiction, yet her words seem singularly apt. The addict knows no happiness. Perversion of the soul by drugs is truly a disaster, and one that parents more than others may be able to forestall.

What parents can do

Probably the most important action that *individual* parents can take to reduce the risk of addiction is to bring their children up in a stable home, and to give them all kinds of opportunities for developing a sense of judgement—by joining in every type of activity, making their own decisions and learning progressively from their own mistakes. The teenager exposed to an offer of drugs is on his own; he will be most likely to refuse it if he can make up his own mind that the risk is not worthwhile. To do this he needs to know just as much about drug-taking as about drink or sex. These rather obvious features of a sensible upbringing may do more than anything else to reduce susceptibility.

Provided with a positive interest in life—and independence when they are ready for it—most teenagers feel little need of drugs. However, some are less stable. Their difficulties may be apparent as anxiety, depression, sleeplessness or erratic behaviour. Or they may be disguised as physical disease, over-dependence on mother, inability to make or keep friends, lack of progress at school, or devotion to an escapist hobby. In such cases it is often worthwhile to discuss the problem with a general practitioner or the school authorities, Referral to a Child Guidance Clinic (for those under fourteen) or psychiatrist may be helpful.

When the risk of drug-taking is increased by exposure to dubious friends, it may be necessary to forbid *young* teenagers to see them. But as every parent knows, older teenagers present a more difficult problem. In general it is probably best to give advice and discuss problems even if your views are sharply rebuffed. Firmness supported by reasoned explanations has at least a chance of being respected. Weakness is more often despised and stern discipline resented.

When parents feel unable to cope on their own, help and advice can be obtained from the Association for the Prevention of Addiction, or from general practitioners, welfare and probation officers, school-teachers, clergy, or the police. Many have direct experience of the drug problem as it affects a particular locality. All are concerned to prevent the spread of drug abuse. Even if positive action is impossible, talking over a problem tends to sort out ideas and cut it down to size.

Apart from these and other individual measures such as early diagnosis, to be discussed later, parents may be

Parents

able to limit the spread of drug-taking by group action :

—by urging proper teaching on drug abuse in all schools

—by ensuring that parents and teachers are taught to recognize the early signs of drug-taking

—by exchanging information with other parents and responsible people, and joining organizations like the Association for the Prevention of Addiction, which is a national organization with branches in areas where drug abuse is common

—by stimulating and raising funds for research into the problem of drug abuse

—by encouraging the provision of facilities for all types of recreation for young people, with the emphasis on active participation

—by proposing the establishment of a youth advisory service which can be consulted by young people at school or at work without formality or delay (at present they have nowhere to turn apart from innumerable separate agencies not directly approachable or really geared to their needs)

—by exerting pressure for other action, such as homes for those without them, some system of care for young people on the loose in large towns, and any necessary changes in the law on drugs or its administration.

2 The soft drugs

Marihuana and amphetamine stimulants are the soft drugs most commonly abused in England today, and they are certainly the two most likely to be of practical concern to parents. Though one is obtained from the hemp plant and the other a factory-produced chemical, they have several features in common. Both exist in a number of different forms known by a whole range of names. Both are reasonably cheap and easy to obtain on the black market in this country, and their possession is illegal, except in the case of amphetamine obtained on a doctor's prescription. Both alter the user's mood. Marihuana induces the happy dreamlike state known as euphoria, while amphetamine acts as a straightforward stimulant increasing mental and physical activity and preventing sleep. Neither commonly causes physical dependence. Indeed, users often find them socially helpful, for both drugs reduce inhibitions and enable diffident people to overcome their shyness and make personal contacts more easily. The tendency to group use—marihuana for hippies and amphetamine for mods are the obvious examples—is probably due in part to this effect. Psychological dependence develops quite frequently, but it is not unknown for regular takers to hold down a job and lead a reasonably normal life.

What, then, are the objections to soft drugs? The first and most significant is that countries which have experienced widespread abuse are the most concerned about their ill-effects, the most vehement in their denunciation. Large doses may be associated with criminal or delinquent behaviour; persistent over-indulgence may undermine the will to work and be damaging to the personality, and there is always the danger of progressing to hard drugs. There are excellent reasons for maintaining strict controls on soft drugs. But every question has two sides, and legalization of marihuana —which has been repeatedly proposed in recent years— will be discussed later. First, it is necessary to know more about the drug itself.

Marihuana

All marihuana is obtained from the hemp plant *Cannabis sativa*, a sub-tropical cousin of the common hop used in brewing beer. Like the hop plant it has two forms. The male grows to a height of 12 to 15 feet and provides in moderate climates the tough hemp fibres used in rope-making. The female—appropriately shorter in stature—carries flower heads and is the source of a sticky yellow sap, cannabis resin. This forms the active basis of all cannabis preparations. Allowed to ripen after fertilization, the female plants also yield oily seeds used in varnish and linoleum manufacture and as bird seed, but these lack any drug activity. *Cannabis sativa* is a versatile plant, but for its devotees only the resin really matters. It is produced in the greatest quantity and strength when the female plants are grown under ideal conditions in a hot and humid climate, and prevented from going to seed. In the foothills of the Himalayas, where production of cannabis resin has been brought to a fine art, the male plants are weeded out and thrown away to avoid any possibility of fertilization. The men doing this job maintain the superiority of their sex by referring to the poor rejects as female, and the fine resin-producing females as male.

Cannabis resin can be obtained in a number of different ways. One of the most extraordinary and un-hygienic was employed in Nepal where so much sap is produced that it seeps out and coats the upper part of the plants. Norman Taylor has described* how, before the flower heads were ready for gathering, naked men ran between the close-set rows, resin adhering to their sweating bodies as they passed, to be scraped off when a sufficient quantity had accumulated. The resultant dried product, like the pure resin ob-

* *Narcotics, Nature's Dangerous Gifts*, by Norman Taylor, Delta Books, New York, 1963.

tained from freshly cut plant tops, is known to the Indians as *charas*. In the Middle East and in this country powdered preparations of pure resin are known as *hashish*. But the word is often used erroneously for milder forms of cannabis not of such high quality or prepared with such care. Almost every account of cannabis intoxication as a serious threat to society and to the individual refers to the use of pure resin in the form of hashish or charas. Crime, debauchery, murder, immorality and madness have been attributed to these powerful preparations throughout the countries where their use has been customary for thousands of years.

Fortunately, the cost of pure cannabis resin is high and this has always prevented its widespread use. Cheaper products of much lower potency are therefore more commonly used. Known as *ganja* in India, one of these consists of the whole flowering head of the female hemp plant manufactured into 'tobacco', sweets or drinks. Although hemp was specially cultivated in India for ganja manufacture and potency is moderately high, there are few reports of serious harm resulting from its use.

Finally, for those too poor even to afford ganja there is the pauper's cannabis obtained from plants growing in the wild. The quality is variable but usually poor, since growing conditions are seldom ideal and pollination cannot be prevented. Crude methods of preparation often impair potency further. The plant tops are either dried, cut up and smoked, or brewed to prepare what is euphemistically called cannabis resin, but does not approach the strength of the real thing. These poor relations of the cannabis family are called *bhang* in India, *kif* in Morocco, *dagga* in South Africa, and *marihuana* in Mexico and Latin America. Habitués know them by such slang names as grass, pot, weed, tea, and the cigarettes made from them as joints or reefers. It is fortunate that these are the commonest forms of cannabis available on the black market in Britain at the present time, though illegal imports of resin are certainly on the increase. Marihuana is said to enter the U.S. mainly from Mexico and to have only one-fifth to one-eighth of the potency of pure resin. Supplies reaching Britain, mainly via Morocco, seem to be a little stronger.

Differences in potency undoubtedly account for the very wide range of opinions about cannabis. Some extol its virtues while others stress its evils; the large variations between different preparations are often overlooked. It is almost as though housewives were discussing the rival merits of their bread without knowing that some were using the finest flour expertly ground from best wheat, others home-ground wild wheat flour, and yet others ground-up grass seed. Disagreement is inevitable in such circumstances. However, some old disagreements about cannabis have been resolved in recent years. Botanists are now agreed that all hemp plants from different parts of the world are of a single variety —*Cannabis sativa*—and chemists have made steady progress in identifying the active drug present in the resin. Although work is by no means complete, there is now no doubt that cannabis resin owes most of its activity to a mixture of tetrahydrocannabinols (THC). At least three isomers—compounds made up of the same atoms differently arranged—have been found. The quantities of each vary widely according to the source, method of preparation and 'vintage' of the sample. Some seasons are better than others for cannabis resin, just as they are for wine.

Cannabis preparations contain additional compounds chemically similar to THC. Most of them have no direct euphoric effect, but cannabidiolic acid is a sedative with some anti-bacterial activity, and others turn into forms of THC when heated in the presence of oxygen. Because of this, the act of smoking hemp must increase its potency. No wonder smoking is so widely preferred to eating hemp products. Reefer cigarettes are favoured in the West, large marihuana cigars for communal smoking in Mexico, and sometimes the hookah or hubble-bubble pipe in the Middle East. Although the practice may be declining, the communal reefer, cigar or hookah passed from mouth to mouth among a group of smokers is typical of the sociable atmosphere engendered by the drug and important for its full enjoyment.

Even with a standardized preparation which is still being developed, the effects of smoking hemp cannot be accurately evaluated in the laboratory. Much depends on the character, mood, and expectations of the smoker and his friends. 'Idiosyncrasy may not be the star performer,' wrote the American physician Victor Robinson early this century, 'but it certainly plays an important part . . . No drug in the entire *materia medica* is capable of producing such a diversity of effects.' The action of cannabis is almost instantaneous as the smoke enters the bloodstream directly from the mouth, throat and lungs, the breath being held after each inhalation for maximum effect.

With his inhibitions released the subject becomes, in a sense, more himself. The active, the intellectual, the lecherous, the violent, the sociable, even the morose, all tend to become caricatures of themselves, yet infected with a happy dreamlike euphoria, which usually damps down aggression. The effect is by no means always the same for a particular smoker. Much depends on his previous mood and thoughts. He and his companions can even steer the experience one way or another. The smoker's sense of space is commonly distorted, and he may—like Alice in Wonderland—be anxious about the plight of his own body. Time becomes extended, so that each passing moment can be held and savoured to the full. What seem to the onlooker to be disjointed scraps of garrulous, inane or humorous conversation are part of a grand hallucination in the smoker's mind. Everything seems easy. He can write great books, paint great pictures, dance, make love, drive a sports car, do almost anything better, more quickly, more successfully and with more enjoyment than ever before. He is convinced he can, but he seldom does. Instead he goes on smoking and dreaming. Talkative and silent by turns, he may eventually fall asleep.

It is hard to give a more precise account of cannabis intoxication. At the end of the last century the French psychiatrist Moreau came close to one with a list of his own symptoms under the influence of the drug. First, there was a feeling of well-being, then disturbance of thought-concentration, altered perception of time and place, followed by increased sensitivity of hearing, delirium and finally illusions. Very large doses induce weird hallucinations like those brought on by LSD. The physical effects are more definite. Marihuana reddens the eyes, dries the mouth, improves appetite and relieves pain; the blood sugar level and body temperature fall, urinary output, pulse rate and blood pressure all rise. Both the mental and physical effects of the drug last for at least four or five hours and then wear off gradually—much as with alcohol—according to the size of the dose taken. Some enthusiasts claim that hangover never follows intoxication, but this is certainly an exaggeration. In fact, a 'let-down' feeling, headache, sleepiness and inability to work with normal speed or accuracy are not uncommon after-effects.

Despite all the uncertainties about marihuana, one thing at least is clear. Occasional small doses of a mild preparation are most unlikely to do any serious physical, mental or social harm. To this extent parents can be reassured, and campaigns to legalize its use may appear to be justified. On the other hand, for some people the drug is indubitably habit-forming. Dosage cannot be relied upon to remain either small or occasional. Though cannabis preparations lose their effect for regular takers only very slowly—tolerance is not marked —a taste may be acquired for frequent use and large hallucination-producing doses.

Since time immemorial, preparations of cannabis resin have been used in medical treatment. As soporifics, sedatives and anaesthetics, for the relief of pain and madness, and in the therapy of almost every imaginable disease, they have only recently dropped out of use. Medical preparations known as *Cannabis indica* or tincture of cannabis are still listed in some European pharmacopoeias today. It is doubtful if they are ever prescribed, for their strength and effect vary unpredictably. Better drugs are available for every condition in which they were once found useful. Cannabis preparations as such have no place in modern medicine, though research could yet find uses for individual chemical constituents of the resin. The only 'use' for cannabis in western countries today is abuse.

Serious abuse takes two main forms. Acute hashish intoxication is the most dramatic, is generally caused only by pure resin, and seems to be rare even in countries where this is available. Reports describe extreme delirium and agitation, in which some smokers are liable to commit acts of criminal or sexual violence before falling into a deep stupor. Recovery takes several days. This—the classic picture of the hashish-crazed assassin—contrasts sharply with the passive user of milder preparations like marihuana.

The second form of serious abuse is habitual intoxication. In this, consumption varies greatly from country to country, five to eight reefers daily being usual in the U.S.A., while an Indian habitué might consume charas equivalent in strength to fifty or even one hundred reefers each day. Here we come up against the conflicts of opinion already mentioned. Does habitual intoxication ruin health or do no harm? Does it stimulate sexual activity or damp down desire? Does it stop people working or help them do so? Does it ruin life or make harsh conditions more tolerable? Does it bring on madness or give protection from it? Does it cause crime and violence or make the smoker too

34

lethargic to bother? Responsible authorities backed by impressive evidence are ranged on each side of every one of these questions. Cannabis can do all these things. According to the circumstances, it can be the poor man's heaven or a road to hell on earth. Its effect depends mainly on the preparation used, but also on the amount taken, the smoker's personality and mood, the company he keeps and the whole social situation. But one factor—the potency of the preparation—is of overriding importance. Hashish and charas can be extremely harmful, marihuana very much less so. Some authorities doubt whether occasional smoking of mild preparations should be classed as abuse at all.

Assessing the potency of cannabis preparations presents some difficulty. It is hard to measure even in a modern laboratory, and almost impossible for the smoker to estimate with any accuracy. This difficulty is said to be overcome in a particularly attractive way in Mexico. The smokers sit in a circle around a sacred iguana, a type of lizard. As a large marihuana cigar is passed from mouth to mouth, the iguana follows with its own wide open to inhale the smoke. When it finally collapses the smokers know that it is time for them to stop. Elsewhere such measures are not available. Marihuana smokers can only guess the strength of a reefer by its flavour and effects. Considerable experience is required to control the dose while being intoxicated by it.

Amongst all this uncertainty, it is generally agreed that physical dependence upon cannabis is rare and not severe when it does occur. After years of large doses the drug can be stopped abruptly in most cases without any serious physical effects. Psychological dependence is another matter. The habitué may be most unwilling to give up the pleasant effects of cannabis intoxication. Is this true addiction? Has he 'given himself up to the drug'? Again, the experts disagree, though most would reply 'no'; again, the answer depends largely on the quantity and potency of the product consumed.

Finally, there is the question of progression. Is cannabis a stepping-stone to serious addiction with morphine or heroin? In countries where hemp products are an accepted part of life, they seem to provide a satisfactory outlet that loses little of its effect as time goes by. For most users there is no need to change. Cannabis intoxication is well suited to a hot climate and harsh conditions. Unlike alcohol, the drug was not expressly forbidden by Mohammed, with the result that it is widely used throughout the Moslem world today. Moreover, it is highly prized in the East, like opium-smoking, as a means of attaining passivity. In Western society with its emphasis on frenetic activity the situation is otherwise. Habit-forming drugs are used more often to 'turn on' and 'get with it' than to contract out. A proportion of marihuana smokers here and in the U.S. begin to look round for something more exciting. A few find it in hard drugs like heroin.

Marihuana smoking has only become widespread in Britain during the past decade. The idea of smoking it seems to have travelled from Mexico via the United States or arrived with coloured immigrants. Entertainers and jazz musicians, abetted by students, writers, and immigrants from Africa, Asia or the Caribbean, seem to have been mainly responsible. The role of organized crime is uncertain. It must play a part—probably a very major one—in the present importation of marihuana 'by the sackful', as one observer has put it. But there may have been no need for criminal pushers to build up trade in the first place.

Once marihuana gets a foot-hold, spread tends to be rapid, for users actively recruit others to their 'tea' parties. Many have little sense of doing anything wrong and regard the drug as harmless. Most use it intermittently, much as others might spend an occasional evening out drinking. A few, as with alcohol, develop a habit and become psychologically dependent. These are the really susceptible individuals. Many are lonely because they have left home and lost a satisfactory relationship with their parents without finding a substitute. If they are anxious, depressed, unable to cope with life because of inadequate or disordered personality, or just plain lonely, marihuana may fill a need, however inadequately. Were it to make symptoms worse, life even less tolerable, the establishment of a habit would be highly unlikely; but marihuana seldom has such effects. It is smoked for pleasurable relaxation (sometimes in larger quantities for hallucinations) and almost always produces the illusion that it did some good. In any event, most susceptible teenagers have little or no insight into their own psychological needs and inadequacies. They are attracted by membership of a group and find that they like what the group has to offer.

Marihuana is widely believed to be harmless, and even well-known psychiatrists have campaigned for its use to be made legal. The situation is perfect for any normally rebellious teenager. He or she can break the law, shock parents and impress friends with revelations about drug-taking, derive a good deal of pleasure from membership of the group, and from marihuana itself—all for no risk, or just enough to be exciting. No wonder the habit spreads so rapidly.

Many different types of groups and individuals are likely to be involved in Britain at the present time. They include hippies, flower people (or whatever the fashionable equivalent may be called), pop stars and their fans, jazz musicians, anyone concerned with show-business, students at universities, technical colleges and even at school, campaigners for nuclear disarmament and other protesters, artists and literary people, frequenters of coffee bars, clubs and low dives, factory workers in their teens and twenties, and idlers rich and poor. The pattern varies from place to place and from time to time. Even pre-teenage children have occasionally been involved; in June 1968 a twelve-year-old schoolgirl was found smoking a reefer. Possible users can sometimes be identified by eccentric clothes and hair styles, though many of these are harmless enough—'plastic hippies', as the Americans call them.

At present marihuana is most commonly smoked in large towns, but there is evidence of spread to smaller communities and summer resorts, where it can be bought without difficulty. Obtaining supplies presents no problem for those in the know. Since there is as yet no fixed pattern of marihuana use the groups involved may change quite rapidly. However, parents can probably spot the likely users in their own locality if they keep an eye on the local paper, exchange information with one another, and discuss the question with their own teenagers. More than that, parents' organizations could well arrange discussions and meetings with police, schoolteachers and other responsible authorities.

Apart from the points already mentioned, there is much to be said for prevention. Marihuana-smoking carries distinct risks which have little to do with the merits or dangers of the drug itself. First, reefers are of variable strength and purity; there is a widespread impression among users that some are adulterated with opium, which would be difficult or impossible for the smoker to detect. Second, the smoking group may have highly undesirable criminal or sexual associations. Third, some members of the group may be using other drugs—amphetamines, heroin or cocaine, LSD—and try to introduce the marihuana-smoker to them. This may be a 'social' rather than a criminal offer by a pedlar, but is none the less dangerous for that. Fourth, possession of any cannabis product is illegal and prosecutions for this offence are increasing.

Though it is arguable that some of these disadvantages would disappear if marihuana-smoking were legalized, the present law takes a serious view of the habit—classing all cannabis products with the hard drugs. The Dangerous Drugs Act of 1965 lays down maximum sentences ranging from a £250 fine or twelve months imprisonment up to £1,000 or ten years, according to the gravity of the offence. In practice, sentences have been very much lower than this for unauthorized possession of a few reefers, but can be harsher when illegal importation contravenes the Customs and Excise Act as well. An Indian space scientist, convicted at the Old Bailey in September 1968 of illegally importing over 400 lbs of cannabis resin, was fined £2,000 and sent to prison for five years.

The offences listed in the Act include unauthorized import, export, production, sale or distribution—even knowingly cultivating a cannabis plant—in addition to the better known offence of unauthorized possession. It is equally an offence for an occupier to permit smoking or dealing in cannabis on his premises. Curiously, the law is even stricter where management of premises is concerned. Whereas an occupier commits an offence only if he knows what is going on, any person concerned in managing premises used for smoking or dealing in cannabis can be convicted whether he knows or not. (This is what happened in the Sweet case in 1968 —a schoolmistress who had let her flat initially being found guilty of an offence because her tenants had cannabis in their possession.) Finally, it is an offence to attempt to smoke cannabis or to incite others to do so, even if the attempt fails.

If a constable suspects that an offence may have been committed, he is empowered without warrant to search any person or vehicle thought to be concerned and to seize any relevant evidence. A warrant is required before the police can enter and search premises, but a suspect can be arrested without warrant if the constable believes that he may abscond or cannot obtain his correct name and address. Apart from actual arrest, the police have powers to detain a suspect for the purpose of searching him.

Are such comprehensive laws necessary? Might it be

better to legalize the use of marihuana? Before going into the pros and cons of legalization, two further points of direct concern to parents must be considered —how to spot marihuana use and what to do about it. Complete prevention may be too much to hope for in present circumstances. Apart from finding reefers or other direct evidence, the obvious signs are three: red eyes, brown-stained fingers, and an acrid bonfire smell which clings to clothes for days. There are as yet no medical methods of diagnosis and no routine tests for detection of marihuana in blood or urine. Dry cough, thirst and increased appetite, unusual or erratic behaviour, dubious friends, may help to complete the picture. Spotting even the occasional smoker should not be too difficult if he or she is still living at home.

Treatment, on the other hand, hardly exists. As the drug can be stopped without physical ill-effects in most cases there is no medical problem. Some teenage marihuana-smokers have psychological difficulties, in which case these rather than the drug habit require attention. Many are making nothing more than a fairly harmless teenage protest, which they would soon grow out of anyway. But between these two groups are those with mixed social and psychological problems. Not bad enough to need psychiatric help, yet a little too inadequate to cope with life on their own, they need assistance but usually end up by getting none. Even parents who try to help risk being rebuffed. However, relatively simple measures—frank discussion of the teenager's problems, reasoned explanation of the case against marihuana, even a more suitable job, a change of environment or friends—all these may be helpful, though they may best be carried out in some cases by someone other than the parents.

All in all, one is left with the feeling that society has not yet learned to cope with the problems of its mildly inadequate members who take to drugs. The piecemeal efforts of parents, teachers, doctors, clergy, welfare officers, psychiatrists, psychologists and others, badly need to be co-ordinated into some kind of youth-counselling service, and some form of probation to enforce abstinence might be desirable in some cases.

The case for legalizing marihuana is simple and deceptively straightforward. The drug gives pleasure, provides a pleasant form of relaxation, does little harm —certainly less than alcohol, according to its supporters —leaves no hangover and is not seriously habit-forming. According to this argument, there is simply no reason for marihuana to be banned. Liberal principles suggest that the law should be changed, since it is already in disrepute through being constantly broken. Readers should by now have no difficulty in spotting the defects in this over-simplified argument. Unfortunately, its very simplicity makes a direct appeal to liberal-minded idealists, who often neglect to study the details. The case for continuing to ban marihuana, at least at present, is overwhelming. Nearly every country where cannabis forms part of the traditional social scene is endeavouring more or less energetically to curtail its use.

Legalization in Britain would be wholly irresponsible at the present time. It could be considered in the future only on something like the following terms:

1. Research to produce a form of marihuana of standardized potency.
2. Controlled trials in individuals of different types to determine the mental and physical effects of this standard product on working capacity, ability to lead a normal life, release of aggressive, sexual or criminal tendencies, and liability to habit formation.

To clarify these points would require at least ten years research, perhaps much more. If the results were satisfactory, legalization could become a matter for the government, who would probably proceed as follows:

3. Control of production and importation extending from the cultural conditions of the hemp plant to final manufacture of standardized marihuana.
4. Laws to govern distribution, as in the case of tobacco and alcohol, and to prevent sale to young persons.
5. Periodic checks to ensure that the preparation was of correct strength and free from adulteration with other habit-forming drugs such as opium.

These governmental controls would almost certainly lead to:

6. Punitive taxation to provide revenue and prevent a wholesale changeover from tobacco and alcohol to marihuana.

Whether the idealists would want legalization on these terms remains to be seen. In fact they are not likely to get it at all. Marihuana grown in this country is usually of poor quality, and the World Health Organization, which frowns on all kinds of cannabis production, is trying to stamp it out elsewhere. Legalization here would therefore also depend on:

7. A change in World Health Organization policy towards cannabis.

It is just conceivable, despite these considerable hurdles, that the use of marihuana might eventually become legal in Britain. Even then there would be some risk of creating a new community addiction not just to rival alcoholism but in addition to it. There is certainly no case for legalization before proper research has been carried out. In the meanwhile, there is a good deal to be said for two changes in the law. First, young people need the protection of sterner penalties for supplying cannabis to those under eighteen. Second, the law at present makes no distinction between unauthorized possession of heroin and of marihuana. In view of the greater dangers of heroin addiction, this is quite unrealistic. Though lower penalties for marihuana possession have been proposed by various bodies, it might be better to let these stand and impose heavier penalties for unauthorized possession of heroin. Either way, such changes would be a great deal more logical than ill-considered campaigns for legalization of marihuana.*

Amphetamines

The amphetamines are stimulants. In keeping with their mundane origin in a chemical process they lack both the glamour and the exotic effects of marihuana. The first amphetamine compounds were discovered

* Similar conclusions have been reached in the report of the Wootton Committee.

nearly forty years ago and several different types are now employed in medicine. None of them can be obtained legally in Britain without prescription. Since they are all pure substances whose composition and effects are known, it is possible—in contrast with marihuana—to give a relatively straightforward, factual account of them.

All amphetamines are chemically related to adrenaline, the body hormone normally released by the adrenal glands in immediate response to anger, fear or indeed any acute emergency. By its action adrenaline prepares the angry or frightened individual for fight or flight. Almost instantaneously the brain is alerted for action, the heart and breathing are stimulated and the muscles toned up. Inessentials like digestion are suppressed; the mouth goes dry. Being designed to help the body to deal at once with any serious threat, adrenaline action is short and sharp. As soon as danger is over, the stimulant effect passes off almost as rapidly as it came, often within minutes.

Amphetamine compounds mimic some of the actions of adrenaline not for minutes but for several hours, the mental effects being more pronounced than those on heart action or breathing. In particular, the brain is stimulated, mood elevated, sleep prevented and appetite suppressed. Two other compounds bridge the gap between adrenaline and amphetamine, both in chemical structure and in their actions. These are ephedrine and methyl amphetamine. Ephedrine, which was known in ancient China as a plant extract, acts for longer than adrenaline but resembles it in affecting the body more strongly than the brain. Both are used in the

45

treatment of asthma, for instance, but not in psychiatry. Methyl amphetamine combines the action of a more powerful stimulant with physical effects such as putting up the blood pressure. It is available in tablets or as a solution for injection.

Amphetamine itself exists in two chemical forms, but is commonly used in the more active of them, dexamphetamine. In recent years, variations and other types of compound have been introduced in the hope of finding a drug which would suppress appetite without being habit-forming or stimulating the patient unduly. This search has been only partly successful and for practical purposes most of the newer compounds can be considered habit-forming mental stimulants.

To oversimplify a little we can say that most of the fifty or more stimulant tablets and capsules on the British market contain dexamphetamine or similar substances, sometimes in long-acting form. They are now prescribed principally as a dieting aid for those who say they would like to lose weight but lack the willpower. Among habitual users they may be referred to as pep pills or bennies, but more commonly—because many are brightly coloured—as blues, black bombers, sweets, or by innumerable similar names.

Some preparations contain a small amount of barbiturate, which seems to make amphetamine more habit-forming, since stimulant and sedative counteract one another to produce a pleasant euphoria—neither sleepy nor grossly over-stimulated. The notorious 'purple hearts' are the classic example of this type of preparation, which is sometimes prescribed medically to calm anxiety or relieve mild depression. The characteristic appearance of purple hearts has now been changed to try and reduce the illicit trade in them, the new version being a plain blue tablet, indistinguishable from many others.

Used as a slimming aid, amphetamines both reduce appetite and increase activity. But these actions wear off after some weeks, sometimes with the result that the patient—usually a middle-aged woman—ends up a few pounds lighter, but with a drug habit added to her burdens. Other applications in medicine are relatively uncommon. They include the treatment of narcolepsy—a rare condition in which sufferers cannot keep awake—and a few mental disorders of adults and children in which, paradoxically, amphetamine exerts a calming effect. Why it should do so has not been satisfactorily explained. In its normal role as a stimulant amphetamine may also be used to counteract the sedative action of barbiturates, in epilepsy patients who must take them regularly, for instance. Similarly, small doses of amphetamine are sometimes combined with pain-relieving drugs to help improve the patient's mood. Amphetamines are seldom used medically to keep people awake, but they have found a place in the treatment of children who sleep unusually deeply and wet their beds as a result.

For a number of years after their introduction, amphetamines were also prescribed to cheer up depressed patients, but most psychiatrists are now agreed that this action is superficial and purely temporary. It does no real good and, as with obesity, the patient too often acquires a drug habit in addition to other troubles. Fortunately better preparations are now available for treating depression and other psychiatric conditions; amphetamine is no longer needed. Indeed, some physicians have suggested that it now has no place at all in medicine except for the treatment of narcolepsy and the other mental disorders just mentioned. Despite this opinion and the considerable dangers of habit formation, amphetamine continues to be widely prescribed, in some cases purely to support a drug habit. Why should this be so? There seem to be two main reasons: one historical and the other to do with the nature of modern medical practice.

For twenty years or more after their introduction, the habit-forming properties of amphetamines were either not recognized or not taken seriously. Serious abuse on a large scale is very much a phenomenon of the past fifteen years. Use of the drugs therefore built up gradually without anyone being fully aware of the possible dangers. Slimming tablets became an accepted part of the social scene, students occasionally took amphetamine to keep them awake for night-time studies, and it was issued officially during the war to keep bomber pilots and others alert during long hours of duty. Its action became widely known, and until it was belatedly included in the Poisons Rules in the mid-1950s the drug could be purchased from chemists without formality. Since then a doctor's prescription has been required to obtain amphetamine legally, but meanwhile slimming has become more fashionable than ever.

Anyone wanting to take amphetamine—perhaps after trying some belonging to a friend or acquired illegally—has only to approach a doctor for help in losing weight. Seen from a strictly moral standpoint, the doctor should refuse to prescribe amphetamine when he feels that he is dealing with such a patient, but issuing a prescription has become the normal basis of medical practice. The patient expects it almost as a right. Has not the State undertaken to provide drugs? Is it not the doctor's duty to prescribe them? For the harassed doctor with many other patients to see, writing a prescription is quicker than long explanations of how much better it would be to diet than to take tablets. Moreover, arguing with patients tends to destroy the doctor-patient relationship and often achieves nothing. The doctor gets abused and the patient goes to another for his drug. In such circumstances it is hardly surprising that many doctors take the easy way out and console themselves that minor degrees of amphetamine dependence do little harm.

Amphetamines are habit-forming for two reasons; partly because of their pleasantly euphoric and stimulant effect, partly because of the let-down feeling that follows when the euphoria wears off. Consequently a degree of psychological dependence develops in many habitual takers. Physical dependence is not a problem unless huge overdoses are taken with great regularity. The drug can therefore be stopped without danger, although some slight physical changes persist after its withdrawal. The patterns of electrical activity in the brain, for instance, may take weeks to return to normal after stopping the drug. When psychological dependence results from medical treatment, as it often does in middle-aged women, little harm is done provided the dose stays within the normal range of two or three tablets taken daily. Even if tolerance develops, the number of tablets taken often rises quite slowly and —though undesirable—this may also be reasonably safe. The patient can lead a normal life. In a minority of cases, however, and especially among illicit users, the situation is altogether different.

Serious abuse of amphetamines in this country follows two main patterns, intermittent and habitual. Intermittent abusers are commonly teenagers who want to live it up at a party. In the extreme case— mostly in large towns or summer resorts—the party goes on continuously from Friday evening to Monday morning in clubs, coffee bars or flats. Partly to keep awake and partly for kicks, but not because the drug has lost its effect, huge quantities of dexamphetamine or purple heart tablets are taken. These are not uncommonly swallowed by the uncounted handful, fifty or so at a time. Needless to say, the stimulant effect is dramatic. The taker experiences an initial 'flash' resembling sexual orgasm. Inhibitions vanish and the door may be opened to violence, dangerous driving, promiscuity, crime or stronger drugs.

For weekenders, at least with the first few doses, all is frenetic activity, noise and talk. Shyness vanishes, the most tongue-tied get a girl with ease, music is thrilling, dancing ecstatic, and sex—if it is bothered with at all— freed of inhibition. The scene is often in sharp contrast to the peaceful world of the marihuana smoker who is more likely to dream of such ecstasy than actively experience it for himself. Other effects of being 'high' on large doses include exaggeratedly cheerful, couldn't-care-less behaviour, combined with restless activity, and sometimes a tense irritability in which arguments flare up if the taker cannot get his own way. He also has a parched mouth and may be noticeably unsteady on his feet.

After repeated overdoses, takers themselves describe their state of mind as 'blocked', meaning that they are cut off from reality. In this state behaviour is quite unreasoning, and little is later remembered of what happened under the influence of the drug. When the effect of amphetamine wears off, the taker feels let-down, exhausted, depressed and ill. He craves another dose, yet needs desperately to sleep. In some teenagers the depression of the morning after is severe enough to bring on suicidal feelings and even actual attempts at suicide. Health may be gradually undermined, employment and morals threatened, but intermittent abuse at least avoids the risk of true dependence.

By contrast, habitual users of excessive doses become psychologically dependent quite rapidly. Many prefer methyl amphetamine, but dexamphetamine, purple hearts and other preparations are also used. The total dose may run to ten times the normal or even more, sometimes reaching over two hundred tablets weekly, whereas a patient on treatment would commonly take only twenty-one. A hardened methyl amphetamine addict may feel that he is doing very well if he can keep to a weekly total of two hundred tablets, since the figure can rise to three or even four hundred if he fails to exercise strict self-control. In such people the drug exerts little apparent stimulant action. It seems to be continued as much to keep 'normal'—to avoid the despair of withdrawal—as for any positive effect.

Habitual takers tend to be older than weekend users and—if employed at all—to be working rather intermittently in the lower reaches of the catering, entertainment or betting trades. Some of them initially found in amphetamines a way to escape from their own failure, or simply to keep awake all night as a jazz musician, waiter, barman or prostitute. Recent reports suggest that a new type of habitual user is emerging; some young heroin addicts (junkies) deprived of supplies by changes in the law, consider methyl amphetamine a possible substitute. Many of them inject a solution of the drug directly into a vein ('main line') instead of taking tablets. This type of abuse flared up in Britain during 1968, and the drug has now been restricted to hospitals only. This is just as well since stimulants taken by injection are not much less hazardous than the hard drugs and can bring about permanent brain damage.

One further type of intermittent amphetamine abuse must be mentioned. Athletes, cyclists and other sportsmen sometimes take the drug—usually in fairly normal doses—in the hope of improving their performance or staying power. If amphetamine were effective in doing either of these things, its use would certainly amount to cheating and all respectable sporting organizations are totally opposed to it both for this reason and because of the possible dangers to health. But does the drug in fact enhance the athlete's chances of success? As regards performance alone, probably not. Under the stress of competition, the body's adrenaline production is already so high that amphetamine can exert little additional stimulant effect and may even be detrimental.

On the other hand, stimulant drugs can improve endurance and stave off exhaustion long after adrenaline levels have fallen. Competitors in long-distance cycle races and other similar events are then apt to be driven far beyond their capacity. Their chances of winning such events may be increased, but so is the risk of collapse—or even of sudden death.

However, the physical and mental ill-effects of amphetamine abuse are seldom so severe. A huge dose occasionally causes paranoid psychosis—a form of madness with delusions—but this is uncommon and the taker usually recovers in a matter of hours, unless he has an underlying mental illness which is aggravated by the drug. Disturbances of the heart, nervous system and digestion are surprisingly slight. The pupils dilate, digestion is suppressed, the pulse rate and blood pressure rise and heart action may become irregular, but the taker is seldom aware of these effects. Perhaps it is as well from this point of view—but certainly from no other—that the majority of irregular takers are reasonably fit young people. Their heart and circulation are able to stand up to over-stimulation.

Accurate identification of amphetamine users is difficult for doctors—often requiring blood or urine tests—and may be well-nigh impossible for those without medical training, though there are a few suggestive signs. Most of these are fairly obvious from what has already been said about the action of the drug. Appetite is poor, the mood elevated, cheerful or touchy, the mouth dry, and the pupils large even in a bright light. But these effects last for only a few hours. By the morning after an amphetamine party, the teenager may look like any other after a rough night. He will probably oversleep, feel rotten, have bad breath and marked thirst, but little appetite for food, be late for work —and able to pass the whole thing off as an ordinary hangover. Parents seldom have firm evidence to go on. For confirmation that suspiciously erratic behaviour is in fact due to amphetamine abuse, they may have to rely on finding tablets. With so many different types to choose from—including some smuggled into this country and perhaps others manufactured illegally— proof that particular tablets contain amphetamine requires chemical analysis. However, a parent whose suspicions are aroused by finding tablets in a teenager's room or clothing may find that the local chemist can identify them with reasonable certainty.

Most parents will be more interested in prevention than early diagnosis and therefore in recognizing likely users who might introduce others to the habit. While many fall into the same categories as those who smoke marihuana, certain differences of emphasis are apparent. Lacking the exotic effects of marihuana, the amphetamines have comparatively little appeal for university students, artists, writers and others hoping for inspiration, seeking insight, or searching for eternal truth. If they take amphetamine at all, such people are likely to do so experimentally or—in normal doses—simply to keep awake for study. Some hippies take the drug either alone or combined with marihuana to counteract its soporific effect, but use appears to be most frequent among delinquent or near-delinquent groups of youths and girls. They tend to congregate in pubs, cafés, clubs, bars, bowling alleys and all-night dives. Many are convincing liars. Their dangerously smooth line of talk helps them to obtain prescriptions from doctors, fool chemists and persuade new recruits to try their first dose. Parents can usefully warn their children of such characters and the places they frequent.

Susceptibility is often at its peak when a teenager first leaves home and finds himself alone in a large town. Seeking companionship, he may well visit the very place where drugs are commonly on offer. If he has no room to go to and sits up all night in a cheap joint where he cannot sleep, an offer of tablets to keep awake has special appeal.

The first offer of amphetamine can take many forms. It may come from weekenders or habitual takers, from a friend who finds her slimming tablets cheer her up, from a doctor, or from smooth-tongued pushers who are in it for the money. The offer is occasionally both made and accepted within a family, not only between teenagers but by a mother to her own teenage child. Since the great majority of adult amphetamine takers are married women receiving slimming tablets from their doctor, observant teenagers soon notice that mother is more cheerful and altogether easier to live with after taking her tablets. Sooner or later they may try one for themselves. We might call this an indirect offer, but some mothers actually *suggest* a dose when one of their own teenagers feels a bit off colour.

Maintaining supplies once a habit has been established follows several different patterns. Because amphetamines can be acquired virtually free under the National Health Service and their possession is then legal, there is a natural advantage in obtaining them on a doctor's prescription. All kinds of fabricated excuses are presented by amphetamine-hungry 'patients', many of whom need help of some sort which the drug does not provide and the doctor has little time to give. As already pointed out, the practitioner finds himself in an invidious position. He knows that he should not prescribe purely to support a drug habit, but hopes to keep his patient under supervision and out of the hands of criminal pedlars by doing so. Many practitioners compromise by limiting the quantities they prescribe for adults and refusing prescriptions to minors. But every profession has its black sheep. A few doctors— especially in London—have become known for prescribing large quantities of amphetamine and other habit-forming drugs, either privately or under the N.H.S. Minors are sometimes treated without their parents' knowledge. Since there are hardly any proper treatment facilities for teenagers who abuse amphetamine, these doctors can claim to be acting in the interests of patients whom other doctors will have nothing to do with.

Amphetamine tablets find their way on to the black market from criminal activities ranging from relatively petty offences to the theft of whole consignments of tablets. With outlets in many coffee bars, public houses and dives at a shilling or more per tablet, this must be one form of crime that really pays. It remains to be seen whether more frequent prosecutions for unauthorized possession of amphetamine will have the effect of reducing this trade by cutting down demand.

Unlike marihuana, amphetamines are not officially classed as Dangerous Drugs. Their unauthorized possession first became an offence as recently as 1964 with the passing of the Drugs (Prevention of Misuse) Act. This lays down that possession of amphetamine or a related drug is unlawful unless it has been prescribed by a doctor, dentist or vet for the person in question, or some person or animal under his care.

Offenders are liable to a fine not exceeding £200 or to imprisonment for up to two years, or both. Powers of search and arrest are much the same as for marihuana. A constable may search a suspect (detaining him for the purpose), stop and search a motor vehicle, seize anything thought to be evidence of an offence, and arrest without warrant any suspect who seems likely to abscond or whose true name and address cannot be ascertained. A warrant issued by a Justice of the Peace is, however, necessary before premises can be searched. Occupiers, owners or managers cannot be prosecuted for offences by others committed on their premises. Nor is it a specific offence to offer amphetamine to others or incite them to take it. Thus there is once again no specific protection for those under 18.

Apart altogether from unauthorized possession, amphetamine abuse and crime are quite frequently associated, since both tend to be features of delinquent behaviour. Twenty per cent of young delinquents admitted to one remand home in London had been taking amphetamines. While there is little evidence that overdosage actually causes crime, dexamphetamine or purple hearts taken for Dutch courage give the young delinquent a devil-may-care bravado. Under the influence of the drug, he may drive with dangerous abandon, knock out a night-watchman with excessive force, or use a gun without thought for the possible consequences. In such ways, amphetamine abuse can alter the whole nature of a criminal offence—sometimes from theft to murder. Fortunately, this appears to be uncommon and it may be more usual among delinquents for amphetamine-taking and crime to exist side by side, without one causing the other.

Obtaining supplies is rather different. Organized crime with a system of pushers for distribution must lie behind the theft of bulk consignments from warehouses or en route from manufacturer to wholesaler. On a smaller scale, individuals or small groups break into chemists' shops or doctors' surgeries in search of tablets. Others go to a surgery in the ordinary way and either steal prescription forms from the desk when the doctor's back is turned, or get a legal prescription and alter the quantity ordered by adding a nought or two. Such methods may now be less successful than formerly since doctors and chemists have been alerted to the risks and now take precautionary measures. However, stopping this one small hole has done little to stem the flood of amphetamine abuse, which continues to be fed from legal and illegal sources alike.

Nobody can say how large the problem is, but the annual total of around five million Health Service prescriptions in England and Wales probably accounts for about four hundred million tablets; private prescriptions and theft for millions more. A conservative estimate suggests that these total quantities might satisfy the annual demand from over half a million patients on regular doses or, say, one hundred thousand hardened addicts. With the wide range of dosage between

58

use and abuse, intermittent and regular, the actual total of those psychologically dependent on amphetamines must lie somewhere between these figures. By comparison, strictly medical indications for amphetamine treatment pale into insignificance. They may account for one or two per cent of the total annual consumption.

What is to be done? As with marihuana, there is virtually no treatment for amphetamine abuse. The drug itself can be stopped without any special precautions, but the 'need' for it lies in the whole fabric of life. Personality, psychiatric disorders, friends and relations, circumstances at work and in the home—or lack of both job and home—all play a part. The adult who has found a solution to some of life's difficulties in amphetamine is naturally reluctant to give it up, and always prone to re-start the habit. Only complete recasting of life with support and encouragement prolonged over several years is likely to be fully successful, and this has seldom if ever been attempted. However, parents can take heart from the fact that the position is less black among teenagers. For many of them the drugs fill a passing need. With fewer ties and greater adaptability they can more easily make a fresh start. But, again, there are few places where they can go for help, and all too often nothing is done until they fall foul of the law.

Parents seeking advice and treatment for their own teenagers are scarcely better off. In many areas there are no special treatment facilities for amphetamine dependents and, although advice may be obtained from general practitioners, psychiatrists, social workers, clergy and others, it can seldom be backed by effective action. Once again, prevention would seem to be the answer. In addition to the general measures outlined in the first chapter, much could be done to limit supplies of stimulant drugs.

From time to time the question has been raised whether amphetamines should be banned altogether—even for medical use. As this would mean depriving a few patients of essential treatment, such measures can hardly be justified. A more practicable plan is proper control of all amphetamines and related compounds through every stage of manufacture and distribution. This is already done for morphine and heroin, and —in different fields—for such things as whisky, postage stamps and banknotes. Cost apart, the necessary security measures present no particular difficulty. Much of the present illicit traffic in amphetamines would dry up overnight. The problem of excessive prescribing (perhaps the largest single source) would remain. Here is a field in which doctors should surely put their own house in order.

With many of the present legal and illegal sources of amphetamines effectively plugged, there would undoubtedly be increased smuggling from abroad and perhaps illicit manufacture in this country. It is too much to expect that all abuse would cease, but the problem could almost certainly be reduced to a mere fraction of its present size. The need for action has existed for some years now but little effective has been done. Here is yet another field where persistent pressure from organized groups of parents concerned about teenage drug-taking should be able to get things moving.

Other soft drugs

Despite their popularity in some countries abroad, soft drugs other than marihuana and amphetamine are not widely misused by teenagers in Britain. However, small outbreaks are reported from time to time, and fashions can change rapidly. If supplies of amphetamine and marihuana were to be rigidly controlled in the future, interest would almost certainly turn to other preparations. One obvious candidate is LSD, which has already acquired a following in this country, but can by no stretch of the imagination be called a soft drug. It is far too dangerous for such a title, though not strictly hard either, for users do not become physically dependent. LSD and similar hallucination-producing drugs are considered separately in a later chapter.

A black market already exists in the newer tranquillizers, overdoses of which produce a pleasantly relaxed, euphoric state of mind, and to a lesser extent in other sedatives and sleeping drugs. All these will be dealt with later among the community addictions. Like smoking and drinking, their use has become widely accepted as the social norm, and abuse by young people can account for only a fraction of the many tons of such drugs consumed each year in this country alone.

For teenagers one of the dangers of soft-drug abuse is that they can seldom be sure what they are taking. Tablets or capsules are unlikely to be stolen from a chemist's shop by anyone with sufficient knowledge of pharmacy to be able to make intelligent decisions on

which ones to take. By the time they are sold in a coffee
bar or distributed at a party, they may have passed
through several hands and will almost certainly not
be in the original container. Bought as amphetamines
or tranquillizers, they may be innocuous or lethal.
There is no way the novice can tell, until too late.
Several young teenagers—some of whom had never
taken drugs before—have died from overdoses of
highly potent tablets which they took on trust from
friends without any idea of the possible consequences.

It is unfortunately true that very many of the injections, tablets and other preparations employed in medicine today have something to offer the drug-taker,
especially in excessive doses. There have recently been
reports of young people abusing a nonbarbiturate sedative (trade name Mandrax) in conjunction with alcohol.
Most of the drugs used in psychiatric treatment change
the mood even in normal dosage. Overdoses taken
for kicks can have spectacular and sometimes highly
dangerous results. Pain-relieving drugs all have some
euphoric effect, as do stimulants like strychnine,
caffeine and even amphetamine, which are still quite
commonly made up into innocent-looking tonics. Chlo-
rodyne and many cough mixtures contain morphine
or related substances in small quantities which do no
harm in the ordinary way, but are sometimes taken
to excess for their mental effects. Similarly, nitrite compounds taken by heart patients for relief of anginal pain
can be misused by teenagers to stimulate mood. They
are usually made up either in the form of tablets to be
sucked or small, cloth-covered ampoules containing
fluid whose vapour is inhaled. There have even been

occasional reports of teenagers inhaling anaesthetic solutions and gases for their intoxicant action.

Sometimes, properly prescribed medical treatment slips over the borderline into abuse. This risk is not restricted to patients on well-known habit-forming drugs like amphetamine, barbiturates or morphine. The same sort of thing is likely to happen when patients get into a habit of taking aspirin or similar substances for headaches or rheumatism even when there is no longer any pain to be relieved. Even aspirin not uncommonly causes anaemia and sometimes stomach ulcers when taken regularly for prolonged periods, while phenacetin can seriously damage the kidneys. Though dependence on medical treatment seems to be most common in adults, similar situations can arise during childhood and adolescence.

Many children with asthma, for instance, depend entirely on tablets or inhalers for relief of their bouts of wheezing. The active drug in these preparations is nearly always a member of the adrenaline or ephedrine family of stimulants; mood is elevated by treatment and anxiety allayed. Since psychological factors often play a part in causing asthma, and the attacks themselves can be extremely frightening, some sufferers come, perhaps subconsciously, to rely on drugs for more than relief of wheezing. This is particularly so with pressurized inhalers. Young patients commonly refer to them as friends that they cannot be without; but this friendship can be a two-edged sword.

In the ten years or so since pressurized inhalers were introduced, deaths from asthma among children and teenagers have increased rapidly. Excessive and uncontrolled use of inhalers by patients who have become psychologically dependent on them could be the main reason.

Other patients can also become dependent on drugs of the adrenaline and ephedrine group. Treatment of hay fever or nasal congestion with tablets, nose drops or inhalers can become a harmful habit, and even the antihistamine drugs used in these conditions tend to produce a sleepy frame of mind that some people find pleasant. All these substances and many others are possible candidates for abuse by young people. A parent cannot hope to do more than be aware of this fact and keep a watchful eye for possible evidence of abuse.

When one leaves the field of medicine altogether, innumerable plant products may become the subject of habitual use. In western countries tobacco, tea and coffee, and alcoholic drinks are obvious examples. The principal active substances they contain—nicotine caffeine, and ethyl alcohol, respectively—are reasonably harmless unless taken to excess. Even the major ill effects of smoking are almost certainly not due to nicotine. Similarly, most plant products that have attained widespread use in other countries form a traditional part of the social scene, are well understood by local people and consequently do less harm than they otherwise would. Greater danger arises when they are used to excess or imported to countries where their use is neither understood nor socially accepted.

It is thus not possible to make statements such as 'marihuana is dangerous' or 'cannabis smoking is safe' which are generally applicable. Apart altogether from the strength of the drug, it is necessary to take into account its social acceptance in the particular community under discussion.

All in all, the plant world from poisonous fungi upwards is a rich source of potentially habit-forming drugs. These could have a special appeal for idealistic young people anxious to reject the moral standards and restless activity of modern industrialized society with its chemical or scientific solution for every problem. What more complete escape could there be than into the peaceful, contemplative relaxation typified by the mystics of the East, and produced by 'natural' vegetable means? There have already been unmistakable signs of such a movement; witness the hippy colonies in several ancient Asiatic cities, and the Beatles in their flirtation with the Maharishi.

By contrast, some young people find that industry itself has provided the means to escape from society. They obtain a pronounced intoxicant effect by sniffing the vapour of petrol, lighter fuel, dry-cleaning fluid or the industrial solvents in paint, varnish, glue, nail varnish and many other products. This habit, which is reported to be fashionable in Scandinavia, does not seem to be particularly common in Britain. It can be dangerous because many solvents are more or less toxic. When smoking, the danger is enhanced by the risk of fire or explosion, and because some vapours are converted into the poisonous gas, phosgene, on passing through a lighted cigarette. Control by limitation of supply presents insuperable difficulties because almost any product giving off volatile vapour can be used for 'sniffing'.

People who really want to take soft drugs have an

almost limitless selection to choose from. The law can control the most dangerous and those frequently abused, but by doing this it can also cut down the number of drug-takers in the community. Thus the chances of an offer being made to susceptible teenagers can be greatly reduced.

What parents can do

At the present time, teenagers and even pre-teenage children are interested in drugs and hungry for facts about them. For many young people there is no reliable source of such information. Newspapers and television have excited interest without in any way satisfying it, few bookstalls carry factual accounts of drug-taking, most schools have done little or nothing to teach children the facts, and parents seldom know them.

Some authorities believe that this is right and proper, that all mention of habit-forming drugs acts as propaganda for their misuse. But this view plays into the hands of the drug-takers. Denied information elsewhere, the interested teenager turns to them, receives a highly-coloured and biased account of a particular drug, and feels tempted to try it for himself. By contrast, a teenager forearmed with some facts will often find that he knows more about drugs than the regular takers. He should have no difficulty in seeing through their bogus arguments. To expect teenagers to make informed decisions about drugs, or anything else, without first giving them the facts is patently absurd.

Parental action in this field might take two forms; to give teenagers facts about the commoner addictive drugs, and to campaign for proper teaching on the subject in all schools. (Schoolteachers already play an active part in the U.S.A. and some other countries.)

Suggestive signs of drug-taking are often related to dress, behaviour, occupation (or lack of it), friends and the places they frequent, rather than to drugs as such. Though it is seldom possible to be certain whether a particular teenager is actively involved, early signs that might be spotted are:

With marihuana:
    Bonfire smell in room or on clothes
    Thirst or good appetite, especially for
        sweet foods and drinks
    Tendency to dry cough
    Changes of mood
    Reddened eyes, which may be concealed by
        dark glasses
    Brown-stained fingers.

Marihuana itself varies in appearance, but is generally recognizable as dried vegetable matter somewhere between dried grass and tobacco; it may be fibrous or powdery. Cannabis resin is a dark, dirty brown substance, only likely to be encountered in very small pieces —often wrapped in silver paper and kept in a matchbox. Though police dogs have been trained to smell out cannabis preparations, the smell is not obvious to the human nose.

With amphetamine:
  Restless, irritable or erratic behaviour
  Tendency to oversleep, tell lies, and ignore
    obligations
  Dry mouth and bad breath
  Sore lips which are frequently licked
  Increased thirst, but poor appetite
  Large pupils even in bright light, so that dark
    glasses may be needed or worn for concealment.

Suspicions may be aroused by finding tablets or capsules, though positive identification can be difficult (see
Appendix IV). Parents will also want to be able to identify the drug-taking groups, if any, in their locality. Co-
operation with other responsible people should prove
valuable. But it is also worth bearing in mind that teenagers themselves may know perfectly well where the
risk lies.

There is unfortunately no single source of reliable advice on soft-drug questions. However, in districts where
drug abuse is common, doctors, teachers, welfare
workers, clergy and police all have some experience
of the problem and there may be a local branch of the
Association for Prevention of Addiction.

Though the position varies, general practitioners are
usually in a position to help most. They frequently
have the advantage of knowing their patients, are
familiar with local circumstances, and can call upon
numerous hospital, psychiatric, local authority and
other services. This sounds impressive on paper, but
may be disappointing in practice.

Many doctors regard soft drug-taking as incurable

and the scope for effective action is very limited except in the immediate treatment of acute overdosage or severe mental disturbance. There are two reasons for this. First, there is no treatment for soft drug-taking as such; and second, compulsion cannot be used unless the law has been broken or the person involved is young. Even when an underlying psychiatric condition requires treatment, the older teenager is free to refuse it, and persuasion often fails.

In these circumstances, many young people dependent on soft drugs are likely to go untreated unless parents can take matters into their own hands. Even this may prove impossible because parental help and advice are so easily rejected by teenagers as unwarrantable interference. All the same, a break with former acquaintances and a fresh start in a new environment are worth aiming for. The desired effect might be achieved by discussing the ill-effects of drug-taking, by changing jobs, staying for a while with relatives or friends, taking up new interests or moving to a different district. Social measures of this sort would probably stand a better chance of success if handled by someone other than the parents, but there seldom is anyone.

At present, there are several serious deficiencies in the soft drug field:

Inadequate control of supplies
Ignorance about drug abuse
Lack of support for teenagers who have left home
Failure of the law to protect those under eighteen
from an offer of drugs

The Willing Victim

Difficulty in obtaining advice
Almost complete absence of treatment facilities
Lack of compulsory powers to enforce abstinence.

Organizations of parents and others could do much to remedy this situation. Until they do, soft-drug abuse will probably continue to be an important social problem for which society fails to carry the responsibility.

3 The hard drugs

The hard drugs are basically two in number: cocaine and substances such as morphine or heroin derived from opium. Among addicts in Britain, heroin is almost invariably the major partner in serious addiction; cocaine a minor one. Frequently they are taken together, since cocaine is a stimulant which counteracts the sleepiness brought on by heroin and enhances the euphoria to be gained from it.

With all hard drugs psychological dependence develops rapidly into complete obsession. The addict's whole existence becomes so centred on his habit that the thought of life without it is intolerable. His attention firmly focused on the next injection, he devotes all his activities to obtaining supplies by whatever legal or illegal means seem most likely to succeed. To his insatiable craving for the next dose are added the inexorable demands of physical dependence. The addict's tortured body can no longer do without the drug.

The Willing Victim

As body and mind get used to its effects, tolerance develops and the dose must be progressively increased. Work becomes impossible, family life irrelevant, food and health unimportant. Only the drug matters. The heroin addict lives, and may soon die, for heroin alone.

This is the hard core of the addiction problem, and its pattern has changed radically during the past ten years. Until about 1960, morphine and heroin addicts numbered only a few hundred in the whole country. Most were middle-aged, many had become addicted in the course of proper medical treatment, and others were doctors or nurses with personal problems and access to drugs. Then, quite suddenly, the whole picture changed. Without apparent pressure from criminal pedlars, young people began taking to hard drugs in unprecedented numbers. Supplies were obtained almost exclusively from prescriptions issued by a tiny minority of doctors. Since the quantities prescribed were often excessive (and frequently free of charge under the National Health Service) established addicts had no great difficulty in satisfying more than their own immediate needs. Gradually others were introduced to the habit.

Fortunately, even with the recent increase in numbers, there are probably only between three and four thousand people addicted to morphine or heroin in Britain at the present time. The majority live in London. Many are in their teens and twenties, and the outlook for them is appalling. Treatment, when they will accept it, is all too often followed by relapse. Early death is nearly twenty times more likely than for non-addicts of the same age.

Faced with this grim picture, the government has set up treatment centres in London and some other large towns, and introduced laws to restrict the prescribing of hard drugs. Since the spring of 1968, the new centres have been the only source from which an addict can legally obtain supplies. Reasonable though these measures sound, it is very doubtful whether they will prove effective in preventing the further spread of hard-drug abuse among young people or in curing those already addicted.

Opium and its derivatives

Opium has been known and valued for thousands of years as a pain-relieving and intoxicating drug. It is obtained from the seed pods of *Papaver somniferum*, an oriental annual poppy with white or purplish flowers. Very little, if any, can be obtained from other parts of the plant or from the numerous other varieties of poppy. Though *Papaver somniferum* will grow in many climates, the richest yield of opium is obtained in warm or sub-tropical conditions, from Macedonia and Turkey right across to China. Both cultivation of the poppy and production of opium are controlled in most countries, but illicit growth is believed to be widespread. A complete ban cannot be applied as opium still serves as the basis for manufacture of morphine, heroin and other drugs essential in medicine.

Quite soon after flowering, slits are made in the unripe seed pods of the opium poppy, which then exude a milky sap. This sap is allowed to coagulate, then collected and dried in the air to become a dark sticky substance, raw opium. This is the traditional form of the drug smoked in many eastern lands for its intoxicant effects, and once used in medicine as a crude anaesthetic and as the most powerful means known to deaden pain, suppress cough and relieve diarrhoea. It is very probably the *nepenthe* mentioned in Homer's *Iliad* as the drug of sleep given to warriors wounded in the Trojan war. In Europe, opium was often available in the form of extracts or tinctures, some of which are still employed in making up medicine today.

Injections of opium were a comparatively late development. The first recorded account dates from the mid-seventeenth century, when Christopher Wren experimented with blood transfusion and injected opium into veins. A few others followed his example, but injections did not come into general use until the invention of the syringe two hundred years later.

Only in the past 150 years or so have the active drugs present in opium been identified. The main one—morphine—was isolated by a German chemist early in the nineteenth century. It was soon found to have many times the strength of opium preparations both in relieving pain and in its addictive properties. By the middle of the century, it was being widely used in the American Civil War for treating both war wounds and dysentery. Almost as widely, addiction followed.

As the use of injections spread, the dangers of morphine as a habit-forming drug became more fully appreciated, and chemists began to study its chemical variants in the hope of finding one which would relieve pain without running the risk of addiction. For a while it looked as if they had succeeded. Simply by heating morphine with acetic anhydride, diamorphine was produced, and this had several times the potency of morphine itself. But enthusiasm was short-lived. Diamorphine soon proved to be no less addictive than morphine. Today it is usually known as heroin; valued as the most potent pain reliever known, and reviled as the most pernicious of all addictive drugs.

Manufacture and distribution of both heroin and morphine are almost everywhere controlled by international agreement. Some countries, including the U.S.A., have banned heroin altogether, even for medical purposes, but doctors have successfully resisted proposals to ban it in Britain, where many of them rate heroin above morphine for relieving the agony of patients with advanced cancer. It should not be assumed that heroin addiction necessarily spreads simply because the drug can be legally prescribed. In America, where the prescribing ban has operated for over forty years, heroin addiction is thought to be about ten times commoner than in Britain, even after the recent increase. Complete prohibition, as with alcohol, may have had the opposite of the desired effect by opening the door to illicit drug traffic.

None of the other pure substances isolated from opium has anything like the potency of morphine. The only one used as an analgesic in medicine is codeine, with which many people are familiar as 'codeine tablets', though these owe much of their effect to the aspirin and phenacetin they contain. Codeine is also used in cough mixtures and to relieve diarrhoea. Misuse has occasionally been reported, but this usually takes the form of mild dependence on tablets for relief of rheumatic pains or persistent headaches. It can hardly be accounted addiction. The search for analgesics stronger than codeine and less addictive than morphine or heroin has continued but with only moderate success. Some authorities have even suggested that euphoria and pain relief are inseparable qualities of all analgesic drugs. If this proves to be so, then any really powerful analgesic must inevitably be habit-forming. Certainly the newer pain-relieving drugs of intermediate strength—pethidine and methadone—are also intermediate in their addictive effect.

Since morphine is commonly used in medical treatment, and heroin generally favoured by addicts, the same distinction will be followed in this chapter. For practical purposes, the action of both drugs can be regarded as virtually identical. The effect of morphine on the brain and nervous system has not been satisfactorily explained, despite intensive research extending over many years. The drug appears to be both stimulant and sedative. Thus dogs, cats and a very few humans become wildly excited under its stimulant influence, whereas the calming effect is typically more dominant in man. Most people experience a dreamy, detached feeling of being transported into another world where they doze and daydream in timeless reverie. Not everyone enjoys this experience, which can properly be described as euphoria only when the user delights in it. People receiving morphine for the first time often dislike its effects, needing repeated doses before a taste is acquired. Initial revulsion may be intensified by nausea and vomiting following injection, though this is probably less troublesome with heroin.

The other actions of morphine include relief of pain, depression of breathing and prevention of cough. The pupils become extremely small, sexual desire and activity are sharply reduced and severe constipation is almost invariable. Underlying these effects is the influence of morphine on the nervous system and some of the body's biochemical processes, which come to rely on the presence of the drug and cannot function properly without it. The result is physical dependence. But addicts also rapidly become accustomed to a particular dose so that its effect declines. Tolerance is said to have developed.

Apart altogether from his psychological dependence, his craving for the mental effects of morphine, the persistent user—patient or addict—is caught in a biochemical trap. Being physically dependent on the drug he cannot stop it without suffering unpleasant withdrawal symptoms. And if he continues, the doses must be increased steadily as tolerance remorselessly progresses.

Because of these dangers, regular therapy with morphine injections is confined to patients with severe pain who are unlikely to live more than a few months. Thus the drug is most commonly used for the treatment of advanced cancer, in which mild addiction is unimportant and euphoria positively beneficial. Other uses are all short-term. They include injections given before operations and after surgery, accidents, heart attacks and other painful conditions. Much weaker preparations are given by mouth to treat diarrhoea and dysentery, and are also included in a number of cough mixtures and linctuses. None of these carries any great risk of addiction, though addicts sometimes turn to them in desperation when cut off from other supplies. In this country they have seldom needed to do so. Pure or reasonably pure preparations for injections have usually been available from legal (or illicit) sources. Of these, heroin is generally the addict's first choice.

An important feature of heroin abuse is the fact that hardened addicts frequently take additional drugs. Foremost among these are cocaine or amphetamine to keep awake, and barbiturates for sleep. Cocaine is by far the most potent and dangerous. Being habit-forming, it not uncommonly becomes a regular part of the addict's life, yet always playing a minor part, never as indispensable as heroin itself. Nevertheless, cocaine abuse is intimately bound up with heroin addiction; in Britain at least it seldom exists alone. Some account of cocaine must therefore be given before considering hard-drug addiction as a whole.

Cocaine

Like the amphetamines, cocaine is a stimulant. Unlike them it comes from the leaves of a small South

American shrub. Coca leaves have been chewed in the Andes since time immemorial. No special preparation is necessary—the leaves are simply picked and chewed. The small quantities of cocaine they contain have many advantages in a part of the world where the climate is bleak and harsh, poverty rife and food extremely hard to come by. In the poorest areas life would be insupportable were it not for the practice of chewing coca. The drug increases endurance, enabling the chewer to work harder and longer than would otherwise be possible in the rarefied mountain atmosphere of the High Andes. It stimulates metabolism and raises body temperatures, thus helping the inhabitants to withstand cold. In some extraordinary way that science has failed to explain it seems to enhance the amount of physical work that can be done on a poor diet. As with amphetamine, appetite is suppressed and fatigue staved off for hours beyond the normal limits of endurance.

This is no freak stimulation to be followed next day by reaction and exhaustion. The minute doses of cocaine and other substances in coca leaves stimulate mental and physical activity to such moderate degree that the regular chewer can continue to reap the benefits of his habit year in, year out. It appears to do him little harm. The gentle euphoria induced is just sufficient to make life tolerable under harsh conditions. If the inhabitants of the Andes are underfed and over-worked so that they become emaciated and often die in middle age, coca chewing can carry little of the blame. It can be regarded as an ideal community addiction, so well adapted is it to the local circumstances. Only if very large quantities of leaf are chewed do the ill-effects of cocaine become apparent.

Cocaine itself was isolated from coca leaves about a hundred years ago and found to be a pure white powder—the 'snow' of addicts. Its first medical use was as a local anaesthetic in the eye, but many others followed, and by the end of the last century a trace of cocaine had even been included in Coca-Cola. (Nowadays it lives on only in the name.) Cocaine is controlled as strictly as the opiates, cannot legally be used outside medicine, and no longer has much importance in practice. For a time it was virtually the only anaesthetic known, but better and safer alternatives have taken its place. Today, some eye specialists still employ cocaine to numb the eye and dilate the pupil; the drug is occasionally added to heroin mixtures for relief of pain. Otherwise it has almost dropped out of use, except by addicts.

Pure cocaine is about one hundred times more potent than the same quantity of coca leaves. Addicts usually sniff it up the nose as a fine powder or inject a solution directly into a vein. The effect is immediate and very much like that of amphetamine. Body and mind are stimulated, euphoria induced and sleep prevented. With large doses the user experiences distorted sights and sounds, sometimes developing mild hallucinations. As the effect of the drug passes off, a sharp reaction sets in. Let-down, exhausted and depressed, the user craves another dose. With regular use, it no longer produces such dramatic stimulation or hallucinations but there is little true loss of action, and addicts do not become physically dependent.

Unlike heroin, cocaine sets no biochemical trap for the unwary. On the other hand, psychological dependence and intense craving are common. Doses may not be increased to counteract the declining effects of the drug, but increased they often are—for greater stimulation or grander delusions. Because there is little if any physical dependence, withdrawal is simple from a strictly medical standpoint. For the cocaine addict, as with the alcoholic, it may be well nigh impossible. He cannot overcome his craving.

Cocaine has dropped out of regular medical use because of its toxicity, which may be severe even with normal doses. In gross overdoses, it is one of the most toxic habit-forming drugs. The digestive system may be so damaged by prolonged use that repeated stomach upsets and ruined appetite lead to progressive weight loss and emaciation. Worse still, the cells of the brain may suffer irreparable injury. Steady mental deterioration sets in, and in the extreme case the hardened cocaine addict may eventually be reduced to little more than a babbling lunatic, subject to recurring fits.

Addiction to the hard drugs

Drug abuse seldom starts with the hard drugs. In Britain at least, it is very uncommon for a susceptible individual who has never misused other drugs to accept an offer of heroin or cocaine. Most addicts set out on their road to personal ruin by experimenting with a variety of different substances. Often they serve an apprenticeship, as it were, on marihuana or amphetamine before graduating to the hard drugs. This is the phenomenon known as progression. The frequency with which it precedes heroin-addiction varies in different localities, but two studies carried out in the London area may serve as reasonably typical examples. In one group, all heroin addicts who started the habit in this country had previously used marihuana; in the other, 95 per cent of the heroin addicts had a history of amphetamine abuse. Similar figures have been reported from Birmingham.

By contrast, there have been a few cases—particularly from Welwyn Garden City—of young teenagers going directly onto injections of heroin, but this is exceptional. Progression to hard drugs from soft is the general rule. Fortunately, this does not mean that all soft-drug takers progress to heroin. Very much the opposite; present evidence suggests that only a small percentage of them are likely to do so.

The picture of progression is curiously unbalanced. On one hand, hardly any of the hundreds of thousands of soft-drug takers join the small band of about three or four thousand heroin addicts; on the other, the great majority of addicts once took soft drugs. The reasons for this paradox are not fully understood. They clearly have to do with the susceptibility of the individual and the likelihood of receiving an offer. Yet all habitual soft-drug takers are to some extent susceptible to a drug habit, and heroin is quite commonly on offer in the circles they frequent. Why, in these circumstances, should they so frequently refuse it? There seem to be two main reasons. First, marihuana or amphetamine already fill the user's need —however inadequately—and appear to be reasonably safe. Second, heroin has a justifiably evil reputation among soft-drug takers, many of whom have seen the ruin that follows its use.

The soft-drug taker who accepts an offer of heroin must have quite exceptional motives for doing so. We may never know precisely what they are, for established addicts are the only people who can tell us. As much for their own self-respect as to impress others, they naturally tend to conceal any discreditable motives, and are notoriously unreliable witnesses anyway. However, by putting together the opinions of various workers in the field it is possible to obtain a picture of at least some of the factors that can increase susceptibility to the point where an offer of heroin is accepted. Having tried most of the alternatives, the soft-drug user may simply feel like a change or be prompted by curiosity. Marihuana may have lost some of its effect or amphetamine not be to his taste. If his usual drug is unobtainable, heroin may be tried instead.

In such cases heroin may be sampled simply as an alternative to other drugs. But its vastly greater potency is the more common motive. The greater an individual's problems, the graver his mental state, the stronger the 'treatment' that he needs. If soft drugs no longer provide the degree of escape from reality that is sought, heroin can and does. Unlike marihuana, it packs a real punch. A teenager who has been abusing soft drugs for years may eventually come to regard

83

them as kid stuff; he then progresses naturally to the next stage in the belief that heroin is for men.

Some psychiatrists have suggested that only a person with a highly abnormal personality could derive satisfaction from a heroin habit, and it is probably true that heroin addicts tend to be more inadequate than soft-drug takers. On the other hand, major psychiatric defects are not an essential ingredient of heroin addiction. Finally, the notion has often been put forward that soft drugs themselves predispose to heroin addiction. This cannot generally be true because so few progress from one to the other; and there is certainly no medical or psychological reason why they should inevitably do so. However, soft-drug abuse does create a whole set of circumstances favourable to the spread of serious addiction. Heroin addicts tend to hover on the fringes of marihuana-smoking and amphetamine-taking groups. In such circles, drugs rather than alcohol are the social norm, and heroin is commonly available. Many habitual soft-drug takers become inured to the presence of addicts, even to the sight of heroin being injected. Their natural aversion to the needle, the drug and its effects is gradually worn down. Just as people become accustomed to warfare or concentration camps by a slow process of acclimatization, some soft-drug users cease to see anything remarkable in heroin addiction. All sense of judgement may eventually be lost. The marihuana or amphetamine abuser fails to discriminate between his own comparatively safe habit and the infinitely greater dangers of heroin.

Acclimatization to amoral behaviour is not the only

factor in this change. The soft drugs themselves contribute by impairing judgement and undermining morals, thus increasing susceptibility. Addicts and pedlars know this very well. Always on the look out for new recruits, they find a ready-made selection of the most likely candidates among the ranks of habitual soft-drug takers.

Heroin and morphine can be obtained in three forms : tablets and powder (which have to be dissolved in water before injection) and ampoules of prepared solution. Tablets and ampoules are usually pure, while the powder may be adulterated with sugar or other drugs before being sold on the black market. Addicts refer to heroin by innumerable pet names, of which 'H', 'horse' and 'jack' appear to be in common use. The law concerning unauthorized possession of all forms of heroin, morphine and cocaine is substantially the same as for marihuana (outlined on page 39), though the compilers of the 1965 Dangerous Drugs Act seem to have been living firmly in the past; the offence of managing or allowing premises to be used for smoking marihuana or opium does not cover injection of heroin or cocaine.

The first dose of heroin is usually moderate in size, one-quarter of a grain or less, and is taken by injection under the skin. Novices have to start cautiously. If they were to inject a grain or two directly into a vein as established addicts do, they would collapse immediately and could die. Even with a small initial dose, the immediate effect is quite dramatic and by no means always enjoyable. Nausea and fear may over-ride the anticipated euphoria. For this reason, a number of

85

novices try heroin once or twice and then give it up for good. Others find its effects more pleasurable but do not immediately acquire a habit. For many weeks, they may continue to take amphetamine or marihuana and have an occasional injection of heroin at weekends or parties.

This intermittent use of small doses injected under the skin is commonly referred to as 'joy popping'. Since it at first involves no dependence on the drug, no true addiction, the new recruit becomes increasingly convinced that the dangers of heroin have been exaggerated. Others may become slaves to the drug, but the newcomer believes that he can master it, as he mastered marihuana. As self-confidence increases, dosage becomes more regular, individual doses larger. Imperceptibly the drug begins to master its taker. Injections under the skin no longer have any very striking effect, however large the dose. Something more is needed. One day the budding addict rolls up his sleeve, ties an old tie tightly round the upper arm to congest the veins, and inserts his first 'mainline' injection directly into the bloodstream.

From this point on tolerance and physical dependence develop rapidly. Though the effects of mainlining are striking at first, they soon begin to decline and the dose has to be increased steadily. Since heroin acts for only a few hours, the 'fix' must be repeated several times a day to avoid withdrawal symptoms. The established addict—for that is what he now is—can remain 'normal' only by continuing injections. But he finds that the endless repetition of large doses makes him very lethargic, while the euphoria that was once so intense no longer holds much pleasure. Once again, something more is needed. This time it may be cocaine. Sometimes sniffed up the nose but usually added to injections of heroin, it fills the addict's twin needs more or less precisely—by counteracting lethargy and increasing euphoria. Amphetamine can be used in much the same way. Barbiturates, on the other hand, may be needed for sleep, especially in the dreaded withdrawal syndrome.

Symptoms of withdrawal come on quite rapidly if an established addict is cut off from supplies of heroin. After four hours or so, craving and anxiety about the next fix become acute. By eight or twelve hours the body sweats profusely, nose and eyes pour as if the addict has a heavy cold, and the whole body begins to ache unbearably. The limbs twitch involuntarily, severe cramps develop, sleep becomes impossible, hot flushes alternate with cold. To these physical effects are added overwhelming depression, anxiety or fear. Tormented in body and mind, addicts sometimes emit agonized groans or cries for help.

After a day or so, the symptoms of withdrawal become more intense than ever, with vomiting, diarrhoea, sexual orgasm, and collapse into a restless fever, in which sleep eludes the tormented addict. If he has also been abusing barbiturates there may be fits as well. Untreated, withdrawal symptoms may persist for days, be dangerous and sometimes even fatal. Such is the degree of physical dependence that morphine or heroin can bring about, yet a single large dose rapidly restores the addict to near normality.

The withdrawal syndrome is far from being the

only complication of heroin addiction. Inadequate and irregular meals frequently lead to weight loss, vitamin deficiencies and anaemia. As physical health deteriorates, resistance to infection is lowered. Combined with bad living conditions and depression of cough this makes the addict prone to bronchitis or pneumonia. Combined with unsterile injections, it lays him open to boils, abscesses, jaundice or blood-poisoning. Much of the greatly increased death rate among heroin addicts can be put down to such causes, but there are two other dangers—suicide and acute overdosage. Possibly these should be regarded as one cause, not two. Heroin addiction itself is a kind of slow suicide, which many addicts expect to culminate in death. Whether an overdose is accidental or deliberate makes little difference; it is part of a suicidal way of life.

One rare complication of heroin addiction is singularly abhorrent. Female addicts seldom get pregnant because the drug suppresses sexual desire, but prostitution is a useful source of income and the risk of pregnancy cannot be ruled out. When it does occur, the addict's unborn child becomes physically dependent on heroin. Surprisingly, this does little if any harm to physical or mental development. The baby is usually normal at birth, but withdrawal symptoms begin after a few hours. Untreated, they are likely to be fatal. By giving opiates in gradually diminishing doses these infants can be weaned of their dependence with the happy result that they have a reasonable chance of growing up normally, despite their unpropitious start in life.

Many of the social effects of heroin addiction will

be obvious from what has already been said. For a while the established addict may be able to work and maintain a semblance of normal life, but before long this becomes impossible. All obligations go by the board for someone who lives from one injection to the next. Family and children, if there are any, are neglected. Some heroin addicts work intermittently at menial tasks but most live in squalor and devote their declining energies to lying, cheating and petty crime to support their habit.

In other countries, unemployed and unemployable addicts have usually been driven to heroin peddling or other crimes in order to pay for their drugs. For two main reasons this has happened less often in Britain. Supplies have been obtainable through medical channels at reasonable cost, or even free under the National Health Service, and like everybody else, addicts are eligible for National Assistance (supplementary benefits) and unemployment or sickness allowances. These measures would be easier to justify if they were coupled with effective treatment. At present they more often allow an addict to persist in his habit, supported by the State. Whatever one may think about the morals of this, it contributes little to the long-term welfare of individual addicts. The only tangible benefits are social ones; the link between addiction and crime is more tenuous here than in some other countries, and criminal drug-peddling syndicates have not found it worth their while to organize a large heroin black market.

How can parents and others recognize heroin-addiction in its early stages? As with the soft drugs, this may not be easy. Young people who have already been soft-drug takers and persistently associate with dubious groups are the most likely to start heroin. Behavioural changes, not necessarily for the worse, are usually the first sign. The novice heroin taker may stay out late without saying where, oversleep, lose appetite, become erratic, unreliable or secretive. In other words, he may behave like many other teenagers. But *changes* in the pattern of behaviour should sow a seed of doubt about their cause. The more hardened addict can often be recognized by obsessional behaviour when he needs more supplies and goes with increasing anxiety from one possible source to another. Everything else including personal appearance is neglected.

In both novices and established addicts the pupils of the eyes are reduced to pin-point size under the influence of all opiate drugs and may be unusually large when the effect has worn off. If physical dependence has developed, withdrawal produces running of the nose and eyes. Dark glasses may be worn at quite unreasonable times to conceal these symptoms. The remaining signs of heroin abuse are connected directly with injection of the drug. 'Joy pops' may be inserted under the skin of the arms or thighs. Mainline injections are commonly made into a vein in front of the elbow. In either case blunt needles or unsterile technique are apt to produce distinct scarring, whereas a medical injection usually leaves no trace. After repeated injections, the addict finds it hard to force his needle through tough scar tissue into a vein and is forced to move lower down the forearm or on to the back of the hand. A track of discoloured needle marks may then follow the line of several veins, usually on the left forearm in right-handed people. To conceal these telltale marks, addicts usually wear long sleeves. Girls sometimes cover them with make-up, and boys occasionally have tattooes done over the area.

Since blood often leaks from the vein at the time of injection, small bloodstains appear on clothing, handkerchiefs, towels or even walls and floors. Finally, the addict's essential apparatus may be found—syringes or needles; powder, tablets or glass ampoules; sometimes spirit and cotton wool; less often nowadays a bent and blackened spoon for 'cooking up'. In the past addicts commonly prepared their injections by dissolving heroin in water, using a spoon heated over a gas ring, candle or spirit lamp. The practice is now less fashionable.

Medically, there is rather less difficulty in identifying heroin addicts, since many of them approach a doctor only to get supplies. With heroin there can be no convenient excuse as in pretending that amphetamine is needed for slimming. However, difficulties of diagnosis do arise on occasion; for instance, with an unconscious patient who might be suffering from a drug overdose. But, generally speaking, the diagnosis of heroin addiction is straightforward, and it can be confirmed by blood or urine tests, if necessary.

A greater difficulty than diagnosis is assessing the addict's true requirements of heroin. These are always overstated in the hope of obtaining plentiful supplies, and doctors have frequently been fooled into over-prescribing. As a result, addicts have sometimes had a surplus which they could use to introduce novices to the drug. Each addict *needs* only the smallest dose which will keep withdrawal symptoms at bay, but there is no simple method for judging this amount. Only under fully controlled conditions in hospital can the doctor be certain of the addict's true needs.

What of treatment itself? Treatment of physical dependence is not difficult provided that the addict can be kept under continuous supervision and prevented from obtaining heroin. The simplest and quickest method is to stop the drug abruptly, see how severe the withdrawal symptoms prove to be, and treat them as necessary with barbiturates or small doses of opiate. This can only be done safely in hospital. The first few days are likely to be extremely unpleasant, but the worst reaction is then over and physical dependence broken within a week or two.

A commoner and more easily tolerated method is gradual withdrawal. The synthetic opium-like substance called methadone is often employed because it can be given by mouth and acts for three or four times as long as morphine or heroin, without having such harmful effects. Ideally, treatment starts with the smallest doses—and the longest intervals between them—that will just prevent the onset of withdrawal symptoms. Small cuts in dosage are then made every few days for a period of several weeks. In theory, physical dependence gradually declines until the drug can eventually be stopped altogether. In practice, addicts sometimes co-operate in the early stages because they feel the need to cut down their dose, but co-operation usually stops well short of complete withdrawal. They simply do not want to be cured.

Even when complete withdrawal is achieved the job is not half done. Some slight measure of physical dependence persists for many months and craving may continue almost unabated. Unless he receives continuing support, the 'cured' addict is as much a susceptible individual as ever. If he returns to his old haunts an offer of heroin is inevitable. His friends want him to rejoin the club and he is likely to take the opportunity offered. Only by breaking with his old life and starting afresh in a different locality is there any prospect of lasting cure. Even then the ex-addict would need a home, a job, new friends, a firm place in society and possibly psychiatric treatment as well. In present circumstances, this is more a pipe dream than reality. Such measures cannot be enforced and the necessary facilities are scarcely ever available.

In their efforts to treat heroin addiction doctors and psychiatrists in Britain find that the addict holds all the trump cards. He is always free to reject advice, stop treatment, and return to his old ways—provided only that he avoids conviction for illegal possession of the drug. By contrast, the doctor has no compulsory powers and pathetically few facilities at his disposal— even in the new addiction centres. He must rely mainly on persuasion, which is a singularly deficient weapon against addiction, as Jean Cocteau showed in his *Diary of an Opium Addict*:

To tell a smoker (of opium) in a continuous state of euphoria that he is degrading himself is equivalent to telling a piece of marble that it has deteriorated through Michaelangelo, or a piece of canvas that it has been stained by Raphael, or a piece of paper that it has been spoiled by Shakespeare, or silence that it has been broken by Bach.

Faced with addicts who can be neither persuaded nor forced to accept the idea of cure, doctors have often had to abandon this goal and seek less ambitious alternatives. One of these consists of allowing the addict to continue his habit in a less injurious form. There is then some prospect of his living a reasonably normal life and holding down a job. The addiction is rarely cured but its worst social and medical effects are avoided.

Methadone seems at present to be the most suitable drug for the purpose. It gives the addict no euphoria, not even the masochistic pleasure of self-injection. Taken by mouth in liquid or tablet form it breaks the injection habit. Being long-acting, it keeps withdrawal symptoms at bay with a single daily dose. By relieving the addict's craving it prevents him from returning to heroin (which in any event has no effect in a person taking large amounts of methadone). General health, fitness and ability to work are often dramatically improved. Such arguments make methadone treatment sound satisfactory, but a large-scale trial among addicts in New York has shown that huge doses are needed, and that these are difficult or impossible to withdraw without the addict returning to heroin. Though it is early to judge, it looks as if long-term methadone treatment will prove to be a qualified success which improves the addict's lot but offers little prospect of cure.

Similar difficulties apply to all drug treatment of heroin addiction. No matter how ingenious the choice of drug—one new one acts as a heroin antagonist—it is doomed to failure in practice unless treatment can be enforced. And the tiny minority of addicts who are really determined to get better can sometimes do so without drugs at all. This has been clearly shown by the success of American organizations such as Narcotics Anonymous and Synanon in which ex-addicts give years of support, help and encouragement to their fellow members. Their most important function is to reinforce the addict's own resolve and thus prevent relapse. Their greatest value lies in the continuity of the support provided. The addict has somewhere to turn. Nevertheless, without in any way decrying the excellent work done by these organizations, it must be admitted that they start with the advantage of a pre-selected group who really want to break the habit. These amount to only a very small percentage of all heroin addicts and are likely to respond well to any form of treatment.

Though no precise figures are available, the total cures achieved by all present methods combined may hardly be larger than the number of addicts who would eventually grow out of the habit whether treated or not. This is probably a slight exaggeration, but the fact remains that no method of voluntary treatment has much to offer the ninety per cent or more of heroin addicts who do not want to give up the drug.

For the great majority, treatment consists of

occasional attempts to reduce dosage. Sometimes this is done with medical help, sometimes because supplies are short. In either event benefit is purely temporary. The usual method of 'treating' heroin addiction in England—but not in America—has been for the doctor to prescribe the addict's requirements. This reprehensible practice was always justified on the grounds that it limited criminal drug peddling, though proof that it does so is entirely lacking. Recently it has acquired a new mantle of respectability. Some experts claim that the greatest dangers of heroin addiction come from unsterile injections and uncontrolled dosage rather than the drug itself. They have therefore suggested that addicts should be taught proper injection technique and maintained on regular doses. This proposal must be quite unacceptable to most people. It is neither medically, socially nor morally justifiable. Yet the new addiction centres—lacking the power to enforce treatment—could well be reduced to carefully controlled maintenance on drugs (heroin or methadone) as the only form of 'treatment' that many addicts will voluntarily accept.

Sooner or later public and medical opinion will have to face the fact that nothing short of compulsory withdrawal, followed by many years of supervision and support, are likely to prove effective weapons against heroin addiction.

What parents can do

What has already been said at the end of the section on soft drugs about the need for information and advice applies equally to hard drugs. Clearly, parents and teenagers need to be well informed about both types of abuse. One difficulty is to keep a balance between them. If the dangers of heroin and cocaine are stressed, marihuana and amphetamine may appear completely innocuous by comparison. Indeed, some teenagers already believe that they are. On the other hand, stressing the dangers of marihuana can make it appear more hazardous than it is, with the result that heroin seems hardly any worse.

Drug abuse cannot be portrayed in terms of black and white. An infinite number of gradations separate the off-white of cigarette smoking, the grey of marihuana dependence and the black of heroin addiction. Useful parallels can be drawn with crime. All crimes are undesirable, but not all are equally serious. Parking offences, like smoking and drinking, have become socially acceptable. Criminal assault might be thought of as sharing a middle position with serious amphetamine abuse, while at the extreme end of the scale comes heroin addiction, the 'murder of the soul'. These comparisons are not meant to suggest that drug abuse should be regarded as crime, but merely that both are undesirable and both exist in infinite variety. Explaining addiction in this way may help to keep a perspective between different types of drug.

The seriousness of heroin abuse makes early diagnosis vital. Unfortunately the early signs are often slight. Apart from changes in dress, behaviour and friends, vigilant parents may notice:

Very small pupils, which do not enlarge even in a dim light
Needle marks in the skin or concealment of the arms
Bloodstains on floor, towels, bedclothes, handkerchiefs, clothes, etc.
Unusual drowsiness
Constipation and loss of appetite
Tablets, ampoules or white powder
Syringes or injection needles.

In practice, there may be no definite signs until physical dependence has developed. The addict may then show additional features:

Erratic and irresponsible behaviour
Inability to hold down a job
Poor colour and general health
Weight loss from inadequate diet
Untidy appearance
Tendency to skin infections, bronchitis etc.

When heroin taking has been discovered, what should be done? Ideally, of course, the drug should be withdrawn under medical supervision, and measures taken to ensure that no further supplies are obtained. In practice this would be possible only with an addict willing to co-operate, young enough to be placed under full parental control, or under arrest.

Most cases will undoubtedly be treated by one of the new addiction centres or by a hospital doctor—

usually a psychiatrist—specializing in addiction. The centres can be approached directly or through a general practitioner. They aim to control dosage, supervise the general health of addicts, and eventually wean them off the habit-forming drugs. Attention will also be given to the vitally important question of re-habilitation as a normal working member of the community.

For the few parents with teenagers actively involved, close co-operation with the addiction centre is obviously vital. However inadequate the facilities, it is the one place where expert advice and help can be obtained. Much the same applies to older addicts and those living away from home. Apart from the black market, they have no alternative but to attend addiction centres for treatment. This makes it all the more important that these centres should be provided with sufficient means and proper powers to do their job effectively. Detailed consideration will be given to these points in the final chapter. It may be sufficient to note here that there are two main fields in which parental pressure could help to reduce the hard-drug problem. Apart from general measures like those mentioned at the end of previous chapters, these are: improved facilities for treatment and rehabilitation, and power to enforce continued abstinence.

4   LSD and other hallucinogens

    The hallucinogens are rather different from the drugs so far described. They produce the weirdest visions and delusions not necessarily accompanied by any real feeling of euphoria; the experience can even be extremely frightening. Such is the perversity of human nature that the attraction of hallucinogens seems to lie as much in the very weirdness and unpredictability of a 'trip' as in any expectation of pleasure. It is a trip resembling in some ways the thrills, horrors and delights of a ride on a fairground ghost train. Everything the rider sees or imagines, including his own body, is distorted as though a constantly changing kaleidoscope were implanted in the brain. This effect persists for many hours, invading every thought and all sensations, so that mind and body appear to escape their normal confines. On a good trip, the subject feels at one with the universe, inspired to fantastic feats of understanding. On a bad one, nightmares succeed one another in endless and terrifying confusion, driving him to the brink and occasionally over the edge of madness.

Although LSD is by far the best-known hallucinogenic drug, there are a number of others which should be mentioned. Cannabis is sometimes included among them, but hallucinations are not its main effect and they tend to be mild unless large doses are taken. Among the true hallucinogens, several have been known to man for hundreds, perhaps thousands, of years. The best-known of these is mescaline, which omes from an inconspicuous Mexican cactus, the *peyotl*. Only a few inches in height, the plant looks less like a cactus than a clump of small mushrooms growing just above the ground. These are picked off, dried and used in the form of 'mescal buttons' resembling dried mushrooms, or as the basis for other preparations. Identification of the latter is not easy. Crude forms of mescaline may be encountered as chopped buttons, grey-brown powder, or a cloudy liquid. All of these are taken by mouth, often with sweetened drinks to conceal their bitter taste. Refined mescaline extracted from peyotl can appear as oily crystals, a white powder not unlike table salt, or a clear solution in glass ampoules. These, too, are commonly taken by mouth, though injection is possible.

Mescaline was known to the Aztecs of central America, who used it in religious ceremonial, and it still forms part of the ritual of the Peyotl Society or Native American Church in the southern United States today. Despite Aldous Huxley's enthusiasm for the mind-expanding effects of the drug, its use never became widespread and it has now been largely overshadowed by LSD, which produces similar though not identical mental effects.

The mushroom-like growths of peyotl have sometimes been confused with members of the fungus family *Psilocybe* which also contain a hallucinogen. The fact that the Mexican Indians used peyotl freely while reserving the fungus for special occasions suggests that the latter may be more harmful. Though it is ten years since the active hallucinogen psilocybin was extracted in a Swiss laboratory, not much is yet known about its possible ill effects. If it should be found in this country, preparations could range, like those of mescaline, from crude vegetable extracts to pure powder. All are active when taken by mouth.

Many other natural hallucinogens have long been known and used. The seeds of the piptadena tree were ground to snuff and inhaled in Haiti, fly-agaric mushrooms consumed in Siberia, and 'dream' fish eaten on the East coast of America. The ancient Mexicans, who seem to have had a keen eye for vision-producing substances, found another in *ololiuqui*, the seeds of a local morning-glory plant. In the South Sea Islands right across the Pacific to New Zealand, *kava* was prepared from the roots of the Kava plant, and some islanders still consume it regularly today. Nature provides many hallucinogenic compounds—even the lowly nutmeg can be added to the list—which man has shown great ingenuity in discovering and putting to social or religious use.

At present, none of the natural hallucinogens has

any great importance in England, but the scene might easily change. With increasing attention being given to the dangers of LSD, interest could turn to possible alternatives. A few can be made in the laboratory; but like LSD itself these substances are all similar to naturally occurring hallucinogens found in nature. Two such chemicals already being experimented with in the United States and to a much lesser extent in this country are DMT (dimethyltryptamine) and STP. The first was named by the chemists, but the hippies seem to have been responsible for Serenity, Tranquillity and Peace!

LSD itself has an unsavoury history which begins with the epidemics of St Anthony's Fire in medieval Europe. In wet seasons a fungus known as ergot tends to infect the rye crop. So toxic is ergot that only a few infected grains in a hundred can turn rye bread or cattle fodder into a lethal poison. Before the danger was appreciated its effects were devastating. The French epidemic in 994 A.D., for instance, is said to have killed about 40,000 people by causing gangrene, convulsions and delirium. Even today minor outbreaks, usually without fatalities, are reported from time to time in man and cattle.

Ergot contains several powerful poisons, two of which have found a place in medicine. These are ergometrine and ergotamine, used respectively to prevent bleeding after childbirth and to relieve migraine headaches. In properly controlled dosage they are safe and useful drugs, but in excessive quantities they and the other constituents of ergot cause the delirium that afflicted victims of St Anthony's Fire. From the same

103

basic compounds, a Swiss chemist first made the vastly more potent lysergic acid diethylamide—LSD—about thirty years ago.

LSD is a white crystalline substance of such potency that dosage must be measured in millionths of a gram. A thousand doses put together would not even reach the size of a single aspirin tablet. Because of the difficulty of measuring such minute quantities, LSD is usually dissolved as a weak solution in water and dosage counted in drops. This method, coupled with the fact that the solution is colourless and tasteless, has two dangers. It is impossible for the taker to assess the dose he is getting, and LSD can be given to other people without their knowledge. Sometimes this is done intentionally, but it can also happen by mistake. In either case, the victim is likely to feel that he has gone irretrievably mad and may even be driven to commit suicide under the influence of the drug.

Despite intensive research in recent years, LSD has not yet found any settled place in reputable psychiatric or medical practice. Very probably it will never do so. There is little concrete evidence to support the extravagant claims made for the drug by some enthusiastic psychiatrists and psychologists, mainly in the United States and Canada. The only tangible benefit to come out of their researches so far is that a great deal has been learned about LSD—much more, for example, than is known about marihuana. As with marihuana, the effects produced by LSD depend upon many factors, among them the size of dose, the personality of the taker, his expectations of the trip, and his previous experience of the drug. Even experienced users can never be sure what course a particular trip will take. It may be influenced by the surroundings and by what other people say and do, but chance is the chief pilot on all LSD trips. No drug is more unpredictable.

LSD is nearly always taken by mouth and begins to act within about twenty minutes. Starting with changes in mood and blurring or distortion of vision, the full effects take nearly an hour to build up. The taker has then entered his unreal world, while remaining awake and aware in a contorted way of his actual surroundings. Everything around him changes constantly in shape, size and colour. Illusions follow one another in rapid succession, sometimes exploding into existence with terrifying suddenness. Faces become distorted and weird, walls cease to be upright and may threaten to close in on the taker. His own body is vast at one moment and frighteningly tiny the next. Hands and feet seem to be enormously large and heavy, then so small as to be weightless—sometimes becoming detached from the body altogether. The taker may even have the sensation that he has left his own body and can see it sitting or standing where it actually is.

If the eyes are closed, visual images, patterns, colours and hallucinations continue in bizarre confusion. By contrast, disturbances of hearing and other senses are relatively mild, except in blind people, who experience little or no visual effect. However, sounds do become too loud or soft in sighted people too; taste is altered, touch conveys false impressions and the body may seem unduly hot or cold. Sometimes the senses become confused, so that sound can be *seen* emerging from a loudspeaker, for instance. Time may stand still, race remorselessly ahead so that seconds become thousands of years, or even go most convincingly backwards.

All this, and much more too, influences the direct effect of LSD itself upon the taker's mood. Made madly happy by a delightful vision, he may be terrified or cast into utter despair when this is replaced by nightmarish hallucinations. A trip is not necessarily good or bad all through. Euphoria, or a transcendental feeling of being at one with God, can be replaced in moments by fear or depression. Such changes sometimes lead to impulsive behaviour, which makes constant supervision essential. Without it, an LSD taker on a trip may commit suicide, attack others, drive his car in crazy fashion, or simply be a menace as a jay-walker. Even delusions can lead to disaster if he believes, for example, that he can walk on air— straight out of an upper-floor window.

For all practical purposes, LSD causes temporary madness. Thoughts are so disturbed that the subject is unable to concentrate for long, as his mind wanders and jumps from one thing to the next. Like other lunatics, he may believe that he is capable of great mental feats. Like other lunatics, he is not, despite the wild claims of the enthusiasts.

The best that can be said for the LSD experience is that it passes off reasonably rapidly. After about six hours, the hallucinations become less intense, gradually being replaced by normal consciousness in which brief flashes of the trip intrude. Even these usually cease within twenty-four hours or so, though they occasionally persist for weeks.

An LSD trip gives the user a feeling of remarkable insight into his own thoughts and behaviour. Inspired by this and perhaps by Aldous Huxley's enthusiasm for the mind-expanding action of mescaline, some psychiatrists suggested that LSD might be used to explore the workings of the mind. The word 'psychedelic' was specially coined to describe the supposedly mind-revealing action of hallucinogenic drugs. Research projects were set up to study the phenomenon and find out whether it was of practical use in medicine or psychiatry. The results are as disappointing as common sense would suggest they might be. The most enthusiastic reports were of LSD treatment of alcoholics, who were said to gain insight into their behaviour and thus be more likely to stop drinking. But properly controlled studies have shown that it is not LSD but the psychiatric and social treatment which accompanied its use that should take the credit.

In sober fact, not much is revealed to the LSD taker about the workings of the mind—or anything else for that matter. The psychedelic experience is little more than part of the grand delusion. It does, however, have intellectual appeal. By creating and fostering the whole concept, a few psychiatrists have provided themselves and other devotees of LSD with some apparent justification for repeated trips.

A cult has grown up around the misleading belief that users will learn to understand themselves better. It has even been claimed that psychiatric treatment can be assisted when both patient and doctor take LSD at the same time. Hardly less absurd is the notion that study of the special brand of madness brought on by LSD might give psychiatrists insight into superficially similar mental conditions such as schizophrenia. Such work has produced little if anything in the way of useful results, and has only served to lend an air of bogus respectability to use of LSD.

The American psychologist, Timothy Leary, one of the leaders of the LSD cult among young people, has described the drug as a blessed biochemical, a sort of mental vitamin which everybody should take. Even in this country a distinguished psychiatrist has written in *The Practitioner* that 'few children now being born will resist trying out some form of psychedelic drug'. Though such statements are patently absurd, they do not want for willing hearers. In these and other ways students and others are encouraged to experiment with the drug without having any proper appreciation of its dangers.

Some ill-effects of a trip are mild and unimportant—nausea, vomiting, headache, cramp-like feeling in the muscles. Others are much more serious. Owing to the impossibility of assessing dosage, there is always a danger of taking excessive quantities. In the extreme case this would cause a grossly exaggerated reaction with risk of brain damage or even death. With lesser overdoses the LSD experience is more likely to be unduly powerful or prolonged, and this can happen at times with normal doses, if a substance like LSD can be said to have a normal dose at all.

The chances of the user becoming depressed, frightened or inspired to dangerous acts are increased when the response to LSD is excessive, just as they are when the drug is given secretly or accidentally. Though not common, suicide has been reported as a consequence of depression either during or after trips. Other deaths may have been due to delusions, for instance, when the user believes that he can fly from the top of a building, walk on water or drive his car through a wall at high speed. Such events may be commoner than we think; a routine post-mortem examination would not reveal that a person had taken LSD. Delusions could also account for the American case in which a nine-year-old girl was raped by a man under the influence of LSD who later claimed that he had thought she was his mistress. Such hazards could be reduced by careful measurement of dose and continuous supervision during a trip. They are, however, not unknown under carefully controlled hospital conditions.

Some dangers of LSD only become apparent after a trip is over. Persistent psychosis, suicidal depression or nervous breakdown bad enough to require mental-hospital admission have been reported quite frequently in the United States. That some of these reactions are due to brain damage caused by the drug has been shown by changes in the electrical wave patterns of the brain. This was demonstrated particularly clearly in the case of a toddler who ate an LSD-containing sugar lump she found in the refrigerator. Fortunately, she survived the trip and complete recovery is likely, but signs of brain injury persisted for many months and the wave patterns had not returned to normal a year later. Though this unfortunate child received an overdose, the same is certainly true of many LSD users. Lasting brain damage with mental disturbance must certainly be counted among the possible ill-effects of the drug.

During the past two years controversy has raged around a question which still remains unsettled. Can LSD harm an unborn child? The balance of probability is that it can but seldom does. In theory, there are two possible ways in which a baby could be affected. The first concerns the body's chromosomes, the structures in every living cell which control inheritance. When these are damaged in either parent, children are liable to be born with deformities. The risk is not restricted to the mother or to the period of pregnancy. People whose chromosomes were injured by atomic radiation at Hiroshima over twenty years ago could still develop cancer themselves or have deformed babies, capable of passing abnormalities on to later generations. Whether LSD can imitate this damaging effect of radiation remains open to doubt. Some investigators have found evidence of faulty chromosomes in regular LSD users; others have found none.

The second way in which LSD might affect an unborn child is by direct damage in early pregnancy. German measles and thalidomide are the best known examples of agents causing this type of injury. The evidence so far available suggests that LSD may have to be added to the list. Further research will no doubt settle these matters one way or the other, but airing them may have done some good already. Regular users of LSD in America are becoming frightened of the drug. The fashion for it is said to be declining.

In this country, the 'psychedelic' cult has not approached its transatlantic popularity, but LSD has acquired a following nonetheless. Interest was initially almost confined to psychiatrists, artists, musicians, writers and others. From them it seems to have spread first in professional and academic circles, then to university students, and more recently to hippies, young people in search of a thrill, and drug-taking groups in general. The drug's intellectual attractions seem to have a special appeal for otherwise intelligent people. An offer of LSD is therefore as likely to be made and accepted at university, college, or art school as in a low coffee bar.

Supplies of LSD can unfortunately be manufactured without much difficulty in any well-equipped chemistry laboratory, though the resulting product may be heavily contaminated with impurities and more dangerous than the pure substance. Nevertheless, with doses selling for about £2 each this could be a highly profitable undertaking. The product of a few hours work could bring a total of anything up to £100,000 to its black-market makers and distributors —and be fitted into a small nail-varnish bottle. Smuggling such insignificant quantities of a colourless and tasteless compound presents no problem and must be equally lucrative. With lack of customers the only limiting factor in these operations, pedlars have a direct interest in finding new recruits—a task in which they receive much help from irresponsible exponents of LSD, whose persuasive propaganda extols the virtues of the 'psychedelic' experience.

The Willing Victim

Individual doses of the drug are sometimes available in small blue or white tablets, but are more often made up by putting drops of solution on to sugar lumps, dry biscuits or small pieces of blotting paper. LSD is referred to by such slang names as 'acid', 'sugar' and 'instant Zen', and the takers as 'acid heads'. All forms are illegal in Britain unless given by a doctor or used in research. LSD, mescaline, psilocybin, DMT and related compounds are controlled by the Drugs (Prevention of Misuse) Act 1964, under which their unauthorized possession is an offence exactly as in the case of amphetamine (see page 57). However, none of the hallucinogens can be obtained from a chemist on prescription.

LSD trips are usually taken at more or less deliberate intervals. Doses may sometimes be repeated on two or three successive days, but after that the effects decline quite rapidly, almost as though the brain had exhausted its stock of hallucinations after so much crazy activity. Several days must then elapse before a full-strength trip can be experienced. Tolerance develops and disappears again with almost equal rapidity. Partly for this reason, partly because the trips themselves are so bizarre, so close to madness, habitual abuse for weeks or months on end is hardly possible. The number of users who become so psychologically dependent that they persist in taking regular doses of LSD is slight, and they quickly become unable to lead anything approaching normal lives. The more usual pattern among devotees of the drug is to take planned trips, often in the company of other users. Despite the obvious need for supervision by at least one sober individual to prevent accidents, this simple precaution is commonly neglected.

Physical dependence on LSD has not been reported. If supplies cannot be obtained, even regular users get no withdrawal symptoms. Either they do without or turn to alternatives, of which other hallucinogens or marihuana are perhaps the most likely. By contrast, there is no incentive to take other hallucinogens when LSD has lost some of its effect following repeated trips, for a person who has developed temporary tolerance towards one hallucinogen is tolerant to them all.

Identification of the LSD user is even more difficult than with other forms of drug abuse. There are no signs or symptoms which parents can recognize apart from erratic behaviour and membership of a group which is thought to be involved. The chances of witnessing a trip are slender and even then characteristic signs such as enlarged pupils, confusion and rambling speech may not be noted. A taker might merely appear to be in a dreamy or anxious state, neither obviously intoxicated nor apparently experiencing weird delusions.

However, the action of the drug—whether pleasant or horrific—is often so impressive that young people want to talk later about their experiences under its influence. In this way, the diagnosis may become apparent, though parents could well be the last to hear of it. Almost the only positive evidence that might be encountered is finding sugar lumps in a refrigerator. Although these would show absolutely no outward sign that they each contained LSD, there could be no other convincing explanation for keeping sugar in cold storage. The presence of LSD could be confirmed by laboratory examination.

Diagnosis is equally difficult from a medical standpoint. Even during a trip, LSD produces no characteristic set of changes that can be recognized by examination, and the minute quantities present in the body make routine urine or blood testing impracticable at present, though there is some prospect that a simple test may be developed. In the event of acute overdosage or a highly unfavourable response to the drug, treatment can be given to bring a trip more rapidly to an end, but the doctor must first be certain of the precise diagnosis. This may have to rely on statements of dubious accuracy made by the patient or his friends. Termination of a trip is seldom necessary, however. Supervision while it runs its natural course is generally the only treatment required.

Between trips it is unrealistic to think in terms of diagnosis and treatment at all unless some medical or psychiatric complication demands it. Since doses are taken more or less deliberately, most users feel that they know what they are doing, and can justify it—at least to themselves—in terms of the psychedelic experience. The cunning propaganda put out by American advocates of LSD has led them to believe that they are building a new and better world—not merely running away from the old one like other drug-takers. According to this argument, the insight acquired during a trip can solve the dilemmas of twentieth-century man. It is asserted that not only individuals but society as a whole would benefit; that people could escape from the tedium of industrial city life to enjoy the wide open spaces—of LSD; that the spiritual yearning which lingers in the soul could be satisfied—by LSD; that a great new society could be built on the insight gained—from LSD. Totally absurd and unrealistic though they are, arguments such as these make a special appeal to youthful idealism. Some young people who find conventional religion irrelevant to their problems turn instead to the psychedelic experience. They are not easily persuaded that LSD is a false prophet likely to do them far more harm than good.

What parents can do

The scope for parental action is even more limited with the hallucinogens than with other forms of drug abuse. Identifying LSD itself and spotting likely users may be difficult or impossible. Except in acute episodes, when a doctor may urgently be needed, treatment does not exist. Equally there is little hope of effectively limiting supplies by control of illegal manufacture or distribution. However, many of the arguments used in favour of LSD are patently false and its dangers not inconsiderable.

Perhaps the best thing parents can do is simply to discuss the facts with their teenage children. If the case against general use of the drug is then seen to be overwhelming, the deliberate decision to try it may give way to an equally deliberate decision not to. The pros and cons of LSD-taking can conveniently be reviewed by weighing the likely benefits of its alleged medical and non-medical uses against the possible dangers.

Nobody seems to have claimed any value for hallucinations, disruption of thought processes, and distortion of reality, which are the constant features of a trip. The supposed benefits of LSD all depend on the mind-expanding, 'psychedelic' actions of the drug, yet these are absent or slight on nearly 50 per cent of trips, however large the dose given. It therefore seems reasonable to assume that something approaching half of all LSD experiences can do no good at all.

What of the remainder? There is for practical purposes no evidence that they do any good either. Claims for LSD as a valuable aid to psychiatric treatment rest almost exclusively on the opinions of those few psychiatrists who are ardent supporters of the drug. Instead of conducting properly controlled trials, they have frequently relied on their own and their patients' impressions. Instead of evidence one finds such statements as: 'comments made by patients . . . suggest that the gains are permanent', and I'm absolutely convinced of its value', which seem more reminiscent of television commercials than scientific proof.

The few properly controlled trials so far reported have failed to show that LSD should have a place in medical or psychiatric treatment. There seem to be only two charitable reasons for this discrepancy between fact and opinion. Either the insight claimed by takers is merely an illusion, or it is real but of little practical value.

The same applies to non-medical use. All kinds of benefits are claimed, but where are the tangible results? Ten thousand students in California are said to have taken LSD, but do they lead better lives, get better jobs, enter mental hospitals less often than students who do not take the drug? Is there any evidence that hippies see the world more clearly, protest more strongly, or even gain more insight into their own eccentricities after taking LSD? There is not. The psychedelic experience is little more than an excuse employed by LSD takers to justify their habit. In reality they take the drug because of its fascinating effects.

Research may yet find applications for LSD, but there is at present no clear benefit that could be expected from its use either in medicine or outside it. Against this fact must be weighed the dangers of:

Depression and suicide

Uncontrolled behaviour or acts of violence which could lead to 'accidental' death

Severe mental disturbance requiring hospital admission

Lasting brain damage and psychiatric illness

Possible chromosome faults which could theoretically cause cancer in takers and abnormalities in children for several generations

Direct damage to the unborn child during early pregnancy

Disruption of work, family and health if frequent doses are taken.

The risks are exaggerated by gross overdosage and

lack of supervision when the drug is used outside strict medical control.

Since none of these dangers is particularly common, they might possibly be worth running for some tangible benefit. Present evidence suggests that LSD can produce no such benefit. The Swiss pharmaceutical firm that developed the drug has recently ceased production of it.

5 Community addictions

Most forms of drug abuse are indulged in by a small minority of the population, and viewed with disapproval by the majority. With community addictions the situation is reversed. They are widely practised and even more widely accepted as a normal part of life. This very acceptance makes them safer than they would otherwise be. Everyone knows the strength of different preparations, the size of normal doses and their likely effect. Whether the local habit is drinking alcohol, chewing *khat* or coca leaves, or smoking tobacco or marihuana, social custom and sometimes legal controls govern its use, and contribute to its safety. Thus, drinking in Western countries and marihuana smoking in the Moslem world are both reasonably well-ordered, but if they were suddenly exchanged, neither population would know how to manage them and their dangers would be sharply increased. It may be true, as its advocates claim, that marihuana in itself is less harmful than either cigarettes or alcohol, but it does not follow that it would be more satisfactory in Britain. Apart from lack of traditional methods to control its use, it would probably be less well suited to the Western temperament and way of life.

Community addictions do not arise simply because a particular drug is available. In a number of countries where the opium poppy and hemp plant grow wild their properties are made use of only in local remedies. At least as important as availability of a drug is the susceptibility of a particular society. Only if a large number of people find that a particular drug fills their needs does community addiction arise, often in a singularly appropriate form. Chewing of coca leaves in the Andes has already been mentioned as an example, but there are many others. Several of the natural hallucinogens have been used in religious ceremonies to produce mystical visions. Marihuana and opium-smoking contribute to the contemplative passivity of the East. And in Western society, where nobody seems to have time to stop rushing about—much less to think —cigarette-smoking can accompany almost any activity, while drinking and reliance on sleeping capsules or tranquillizers provide much-needed escapism.

Once a community addiction is established, it tends to follow a traditional pattern with only minor variations until some upheaval takes place in society. Then, two things may happen. The demand for all drugs tends to increase, because people have difficulty in coping with changed circumstances and find that drugs can help them do so, and secondly, new drugs may be introduced. Both these changes have taken place in Britain since the end of the Second World War. As might be expected, the older generations have turned increasingly to the established community addictions (smoking and drinking) and to one that is rapidly gaining a hold (sleeping tablets, sedatives and tranquillizers).

The spirit of youthful rebellion, on the other hand, has led some young people to look for less conventional solutions—marihuana, amphetamines, LSD, even heroin and cocaine. Since none of them is an acceptable community addiction in Britain, there is much ignorance about dosage and no social tradition to regulate their use. As all are illegal, a form of escapism becomes a criminal offence, sometimes associated with other types of crime. For these reasons alone, irrespective of the potency of individual drugs, the case against their abuse by young people is strong. When the dangers of LSD and the hard drugs are considered, the case becomes overwhelming. Yet cigarettes and alcohol represent a threat to the long-term well-being of far more teenagers than the practices normally thought of as drug abuse. Each is responsible for more tragedies than all the hard and soft drugs put together.

Because most people are unwilling to give up smoking or drinking they shut their eyes to any ill-effects. It is mainly for this reason that the community addictions are included in this book. While there are no scales on which the pleasure and relief that they bring to millions can be weighed against the miseries of a minority suffering from alcoholism, lung cancer, chronic bronchitis or dependence on sedative drugs, there are ways in which a better balance between benefit and ill-effects might be achieved. The aim is not to make everybody into teetotal non-smokers who never take a sleeping tablet, but to suggest that the risks attached to each of these things can be reduced by better knowledge of them. 'Better the devil you know . . .'

Sleeping tablets, sedatives and tranquillizers

Most sleeping tablets and daytime sedatives contain one or more of the many chemical compounds of barbituric acid. The acid itself was first prepared by the German chemist Von Baeyer on St Barbara's Day 1899 and named after the saint. Within a few years the first barbiturates began to be employed in medicine, and today their use has expanded to the point where regular takers can be counted in millions.

All barbiturates are essentially depressant. They reduce mental and physical activity in varying degrees and for various lengths of time according to the type and dose of the compound used. The range is wide. Long-acting barbiturates such as phenobarbitone are usually given in small quantities as day-time sedatives for their calming effect, or to prevent epileptic fits. Sleeping capsules and tablets contain larger amounts of barbiturate compounds which act for only six or eight hours, while the action of those given by injection as anaesthetics is intense but quite short-lived. So valuable have these drugs proved in medicine that there can be few people who have never received a dose of barbiturates, and fewer still who have come to any serious harm from their properly controlled use.

Abuse of barbiturates commonly grows out of medical or psychiatric treatment, and is maintained by supplies obtained on legally issued prescriptions. The transition from necessary treatment to outright abuse is so gradual—the borderline between the two so indefinite—that neither doctor nor patient may be fully aware of the change. At first, a worried or nervous person may simply be given barbiturates to meet a specific need. Sedatives to help allay anxiety about a particular event, sleeping capsules to tide over a temporary crisis, are obvious examples. This is the initial 'offer' which most people accept at its face value, stopping treatment again as soon as the need has passed. However, some tend to seek the help of the drug whenever they experience difficulty in coping with life's problems; among them are a few with inadequate personalities or major psychological conditions for whom life is a perpetual struggle. These are the susceptible individuals. They readily become dependent on sleeping capsules and often on daytime sedatives or tranquillizers as well.

Very slowly tolerance develops and the dose edges upwards. The numbing effect of barbiturates on thought and action begins to overshadow their usefulness. After several years of continuous therapy the patient may be no better and no worse than before he started, but virtually unable to stop. Without daytime sedation life's anxieties seem more intolerable than ever. Without sleeping capsules, adequate sleep is unobtainable, a situation for which the drugs themselves may be largely responsible. Psychological and in some cases physical dependence become established. Even if the doctor realizes that he is merely maintaining a drug habit, there is no strong incentive to call a halt. Barbiturates themselves are unlikely to be harmful, while the patient's inadequacy receives support from surgery visits and regular medication. The practitioner, as much as his patient, may be caught in a trap. He knows that help is needed, but has no time to go deeply into the patient's problem. He might prefer to stop regular reliance on drugs, but hesitates to precipitate the inevitable row which could deprive the patient of all treatment or merely occasion a change of doctor. In these circumstances medication of dubious merit but reasonable safety often continues year after year.

Physical dependence can develop with surprisingly modest doses. Four full-size sleeping capsules taken regularly at night are sufficient, and many people take more than this. Beyond early-morning drowsiness and slight impairment of mental faculties, no very obvious change takes place when a person becomes mentally and physically dependent on barbiturates. The patient himself is seldom aware of his dependence, for breaks in treatment are avoided and withdrawal symptoms take the best part of twenty-four hours to develop. Even doctors quite often have only a hazy knowledge of the risks because the barbiturate syndrome is seldom seen; indeed, it was not generally recognized in medical circles until the drugs had been in widespread use for several decades. Yet abrupt cessation of treatment is more hazardous than with heroin and may prove fatal.

Between twelve and twenty-four hours after the last dose, the physically dependent patient begins to feel anxious, dizzy and weak but unable to rest or sleep. After a day and night of abstinence, the hands shake, muscles twitch involuntarily and restlessness increases; the patient faints on standing because the blood pressure falls; nausea and vomiting prevent any food being taken. On the second or third day epileptic fits are likely, and these may alternate with periods of delirium resembling the delirium tremens (DTs) of alcoholism. Without treatment, a few patients would die three or four days after barbiturate withdrawal; some enter a phase of temporary madness, while most fall into a deep sleep and slowly recover during the following two or three weeks. Proper treatment consists of giving barbiturates in gradually reducing dosage over a similar period.

Half a million people in Britain are thought to take barbiturates regularly and 100,000 to be dependent on them. It is doubtful whether many of the latter appreciate the danger of abruptly stopping treatment. Even heroin addicts who take excessive quantities of barbiturates for sleep or to stave off withdrawal symptoms seldom realize that they may be physically dependent on a second drug. The same is true of patients who abuse barbiturates alone in such high dosage that a state of semi-permanent intoxication results. If sufficient quantities cannot be obtained from one doctor, regular prescriptions may be acquired by consulting others privately. The cost remains moderate, with most barbiturate capsules retailing at only about 2d each. Though mildly fraudulent, this practice barely contravenes the law, which has been little changed since 1933 and simply states—so far as the taker is concerned—that barbiturates can be supplied only on a doctor's prescription. They are not subject either to the Dangerous Drugs Act or the Drugs (Prevention of Misuse) Act, unauthorized possession is not an offence, and there are no special provisions for the protection of young people. Yet misuse is common and its dangers not inconsiderable.

Barbiturates rank second only to coal gas as a means of committing suicide, physical dependence on them is probably at least ten times more frequent than with heroin, and many addicts use both drugs. Not all overdosage is deliberate, however. Sometimes people fail to sleep after taking sleeping capsules, wake in a confused state and take more by mistake. Others are victims of alcohol and barbiturates in combination, which can cause sudden death when the quantities of each are strictly moderate. Withdrawal can be hazardous when physically dependent people are admitted to hospital—perhaps in an unconscious state—after an accident and nobody knows barbiturates are needed. Though little research has been done into the personal and social ill effects of taking barbiturates to excess there can be no doubt that family life is adversely affected, working efficiency impaired, and liability to traffic and other accidents sharply increased. Finally, abuse by teenagers is rapidly increasing as other drugs become harder to obtain. Some are now injecting unsterile home-made solutions of the powder from sleeping capsules dissolved in tap-water; the resulting addiction already threatens to rival heroin both in numbers and severity.

In the fifty years or so since they were first introduced, consumption of barbiturates has reached fantastic proportions. During 1967, over sixteen million prescriptions for them were dispensed by chemists in England and Wales under the National Health Service alone. Moreover, a large number of non-barbiturate sleeping drugs and daytime tranquillizers (drugs that have a calming effect without inducing sleep) have been developed in recent years. These have advanced in popularity at such a rate that the total number of N.H.S. prescriptions for them rose from just under fourteen million in 1965 to nearly twenty million in 1967. In the same period, barbiturate prescriptions declined only marginally, so that the net effect of introducing the new compounds has been not to replace barbiturates but to increase consumption of sedative drugs in general.

Does this increase in medication matter? To set against their cost—over £10 million in 1967—the tranquillizers and non-barbiturate sleeping drugs do have definite advantages. In many patients they seem less likely than barbiturates to cause depression and several of them are much safer when taken in gross overdosage. There should therefore be a reduced risk of both attempted and actual suicide. Also on the credit side, many psychiatric patients derive great benefit from the more powerful tranquillizers, which can claim much of the credit for reducing the average length of stay in mental hospitals. On the other hand, the milder forms are most commonly prescribed simply to calm over-anxious people—in other words, to improve the mood rather than treat a mental disorder. This begins to look suspiciously like another form of community addiction.

Use of tranquillizers is already accepted by society and tens of thousands of patients must be psychologically dependent on them. Fortunately, tolerance is usually slow to develop so that dosage tends to remain fairly close to normal, but there is accumulating evidence that several of these drugs can produce physical dependence when taken regularly in moderate over-dosage—much as barbiturates do.

It is worth bearing in mind that physical dependence on barbiturates was not recognized until they had been in use for several decades, and that amphetamine abuse took twenty years to build up. Tranquillizers have become fashionable only in the past ten years or so. Their image could well become tarnished if the sinister combination of mild euphoria with psychological and sometimes physical dependence leads to widespread abuse. No one can yet tell to what extent this may already have happened.

There have recently been reports of young people taking overdoses of tranquillizers at drug parties— often with amphetamine or other substances—and something of a black market seems to be building up. This situation has several dangers. First, the taker may become severely intoxicated and accident-prone, especially if he drives a car. Second, large overdoses can produce prolonged coma lasting for hours or days. Third, many different types of tablet are used more or less indiscriminately; some are much more potent than others and certain combinations highly dangerous.

The spread of barbiturates, tranquillizers and even amphetamines has been too rapid for traditional methods of control to keep pace. In particular, society's duty to protect the young has been neglected. Little attempt has been made to teach them about drug-taking, and such laws as there are contain no provisions —like those for alcohol and tobacco—for the special protection of young teenagers. Instead, they are exposed to more risk than adults, for there is little to prevent teenagers and others from acquiring tablets and taking irrational and dangerous overdoses, whereas adults generally take the same drugs under medical supervision.

Failure to find ways of protecting the young is the most regrettable feature of the spread of all forms of drug abuse in recent years. Parents can help to remedy this defect in a number of ways. These include not resorting to tablets for every ache or change of mood, explaining the dangers of haphazard drug-taking, and pressing for proper teaching on the subject in schools as well as appropriate changes in the law. There may also be a case for greater caution on the part of doctors in prescribing tranquillizers for teenagers, who often need help with their difficulties, but whose interests may not be best served by being 'taught' that drugs are the solution to every problem.

The need for protection of the young is likely to become greater in the future, because of the rapidity and ease with which society now accepts new drugs as a normal part of modern life. There is clearly a point at which use of a particular substance becomes respectable, and this seems to depend mainly on the number of users. Drugs that are medically prescribed start with the advantage of having the approval of doctors and being introduced to thousands of people as safe and well-tested forms of medication. Many new drugs for altering mood are likely to be developed in the future, and great vigilance will be needed if their habit-forming properties are to be spotted before they have been socially accepted. The alternative might be a world in which everybody's mood is chemically adjusted all the time.

Alcoholism

Alcohol is a powerful habit-forming drug which has been so tamed and disciplined by society that it can be enjoyed without much risk. Acute overdosage (drunkenness) and habitual overdosage (alcoholism) mar the picture, but for only a small minority. For every drunk, there are innumerable social drinkers who know when to stop, and in Britain much less than one per cent of the population eventually become alcoholics. Nevertheless, the total number probably exceeds a quarter of a million. Though they are predominantly middle-aged, the early stages of alcoholism may be as common as any other type of drug addiction among those in their late teens and twenties.

Alcoholism is probably best defined as habitual drinking that has got out of the drinker's control. Alcoholics range in severity from those who can lead a reasonably normal life, through others whose health, family, finances and job are undermined, to the very few down-and-out meths drinkers. Like other addictions, alcoholism requires a susceptible individual. In the words of an American, Howard Clinebell, it comes in people, not in bottles. The offer is comparatively unimportant because alcohol is virtually always available, and it is seldom a *persuasive* offer because alcoholism is essentially a lonely way of life. In contrast to other addicts, alcoholics do not form groups or persuade others to adopt their own drug habit. Group drinking and pressure to imbibe too much, to 'have one for the road', are features of normal social life, not of alcoholism.

Most alcoholics are immature males with a background of broken or unsatisfactory homes. Many have psychiatric or social difficulties so that they are unable to cope with life's problems. On the other hand, some are hard-working, competent people seeking refuge from everyday stress and strain or from the memory of some major catastrophe. Whatever the cause—inside or outside the individual—it tends to be a continuing one. Where heroin addiction develops in a matter of weeks or months, years of persistent difficulties and gradual deterioration are needed to make an alcoholic.

To begin with, alcohol is taken intermittently and more as an escape from tensions and anxieties than for any particular pleasure. Gradually the budding alcoholic begins to drink more often and then on unsuitable occasions until the habit impairs his abilities and strains his finances. Worried about his job, short of money and hating himself for what he is doing to his wife and

131

family, he now has more reason than ever for escaping into drink. Life in a typical alcoholic's household is a series of running battles: between the desire to reform and an irresistible urge to drink; between the drinker and a spouse who urges abstinence; between a reduced capacity to earn and the need to finance a habit costing anything up to several pounds a day. The National Health Service provides no free supplies for alcoholics, nor do welfare allowances cover their cost.

The alcoholic is consumed by a constant craving for supplies, without which life has become intolerable; only when under the influence of drink can he function more or less normally. As physical dependence and a degree of tolerance develop, he cannot safely stop drinking and needs more than others before becoming intoxicated. In these and other respects alcoholism resembles barbiturate abuse. The actions of both drugs are similar (alcohol's reputation as a stimulant is undeserved), and people tolerant to one are also tolerant to the other. Moreover, both drugs have similar withdrawal syndromes—including fits and delirium—which can be controlled by giving either. The greatest difference is in ill effects. Barbiturates can often be taken in heavy dosage for years without much harm being done, whereas alcoholism threatens innumerable aspects of life and is one of the most injurious forms of drug abuse.

Persistent drinking can cause—among other conditions—cirrhosis (hardening) of the liver, gastric ulcer, gout, vitamin deficiencies, reduced resistance to infection, delirium tremens, brief spells of memory loss, several forms of madness, and injury to the nerves producing weakness, numbness, or altered sensation in the limbs. Obesity and malnutrition present two further health hazards. (Depending on eating habits and the type of drink favoured, some alcoholics gain weight and others lose it.) To these mental and physical effects must be added unstable and unreliable behaviour with increased proneness to accidents of many kinds. Finally, alcohol imposes a tremendous burden of misery on the the drinker and his family, who not infrequently become an economic burden on the community in their turn.

Treatment of established alcoholism is far from satisfactory. Like other addicts, the alcoholic is often reluctant to seek help, and lacks the will-power to break his habit and build a new life. Psychiatric treatment sometimes helps, but the organization of reformed drinkers known as Alcoholics Anonymous is probably more successful. However, both these methods depend on the drinker's desire to be cured. An alternative is a drug, disulphiram or Antabuse, which turns alcohol into a highly unpleasant (but not dangerous) poison in the body. By itself Antabuse has no noticeable effect, but a person who drinks after taking it feels dreadful, has a pounding headache, flushes repeatedly, often vomits and sometimes collapses without warning. While a few freaks deliberately combine alcohol with Antabuse so as to 'enjoy' this reaction, alcoholics can achieve total abstinence on a single daily dose. The difficulty is to ensure that they take the drug regularly. One state in America has experimented with allowing convicted alcoholics to choose between prison and attending the police station for a dose of Antabuse each morning on the way to work. Though this method has been questioned on ethical grounds, a measure of enforcement seems justified in saving an alcoholic from himself.

Many alcoholics require a whole range of treatment methods. These might include initial withdrawal of alcohol in hospital, Antabuse therapy, medical treatment for complications of alcoholism, psychiatric care for the patient and sometimes for other members of the family, financial help, rehousing, rehabilitation in a job, restoration of social life, continuing guidance and support, and—of course—constant encouragement to prevent a return to drinking.

Fully established alcoholism is seldom seen in young people, but parents should be able to recognize its possible early signs without too much difficulty. The potential alcoholic is most likely to be male, to have an unhappy or unstable home, and to be an immature personality who may have already required psychiatric help. At first, drinking may follow the normal pattern and be confined to evenings or weekends, but increasingly severe hangovers might indicate that the dose is rising. Next, drinking may become more frequent, be used before facing difficult situations, be clearly excessive on repeated occasions or lead to aggressive behaviour. Finally, drinking spirits secretively, when alone or early in the morning is suggestive of actual alcoholism. Other possible signs are stomach upsets, headache, hangover, unreliability, lateness for work, absenteeism, changing jobs, lack of money, arrest for drunken driving or other offences, and family rows. Criticism of behaviour or drinking habits is usually met with dishonesty, feeble excuses or resentment, not reasonable discussion. As a result, considerable tact and patience may be necessary before the idea of treatment is accepted.

Smoking

There are several good reasons for regarding heavy smoking as a form of drug abuse. Tobacco contains nicotine, which is absorbed in quantities large enough to affect the nervous system. Craving is so strong that many smokers cannot break themselves of their habit; and cigarette-smoking has become the most widespread community addiction in the history of man. For every alcoholic, there must be well over fifty chain-smokers more or less addicted to cigarettes. Their habit is far from being a harmless one.

Of course, the risk is not directly to young people. The injurious effect of cigarette smoke on the bronchial tubes of the lungs takes several years to build up into chronic inflammation and a smoker's cough. At least twenty years of regular smoking are needed before lung cancer or chronic bronchitis can develop. However, danger may not be long delayed for a teenager who smokes twenty or so cigarettes a day from his sixteenth birthday onwards. By 35 he or she is already entering the period of risk.

In Britain, cigarette smoking probably causes more premature deaths than alcoholism and all other forms of drug abuse combined, or, to look at the figures another way, about eight times as many people die every year from smoking cigarettes as are killed in traffic accidents. In England and Wales alone, one to two persons under 55 die in every hour of every day of a disease thought to be caused by cigarette smoke. If deaths in older people are added, the total daily toll probably approaches and may exceed 100. It seems reasonable to assume that at least half of these are otherwise healthy people, many of them still of working age. Their deaths represent fifty avoidable funerals every day. Avoidable too are the suffering that precedes them and the personal loss that follows, apart from the expense of so much unnecessary illness in terms of hospital care and lost earnings. The cigarette has much to answer for.

Paradoxically, cigars and pipes—the stronger forms of the tobacco habit—are much less injurious to health. Though heart disease is commoner than average among them, cigar and pipe smokers can reasonably expect to live out their span and die of something else whereas heavy cigarette-smoking doubles the normal chance of falling by the wayside before retiring age. The difference cannot be attributed to nicotine, which is present in all types of tobacco. Though it is a powerful and poisonous nerve stimulant employed as an insecticide, nicotine does little harm in the quantities absorbed by smokers. Novices having their first puffs are likely to experience nausea, rapid beating of the heart, and a slight feeling of elation, but tolerance soon develops. After a few days, such effects are barely noticeable, but nicotine presumably continues to have some slightly stimulating, euphoric action. Why else should smokers experience such compulsive craving? It also continues to reduce appetite, like other stimulants, to limit the circulation in the organs and limbs by narrowing the arteries, and to stimulate the heart. None of this matters in the ordinary way, though a few conditions are aggravated by nicotine, and there is a brighter side to the picture. By suppressing appetite and keeping weight down, nicotine may actually be beneficial, and many have sung the praises of smoking as a pleasantly relaxing habit. All in all, if nicotine were the only active substance present in cigarettes there would be more to say in favour of smoking than against it. Nicotine is certainly not to blame for the two great killers, lung cancer and chronic bronchitis, and probably not for the increased death rate from heart and other diseases among smokers. Some as yet unidentified substance present almost exclusively in cigarette smoke must be held responsible.

Why should cigarettes be so much more injurious than cigar or pipe tobacco? To understand the probable reason, it is helpful to go back into history. When Christopher Columbus first saw *tobacos*—native cigars —being smoked on the coast of Cuba in 1492, they were almost certainly made from leaves dried naturally in the sun. The same no doubt applies to the leaves ground into snuff by Jean Nicot, the young sixteenth-century French Ambassador to Portugal whose name is perpetuated in the word nicotine. When Sir Walter Raleigh and others brought smoking to England their tobacco too was cured naturally. But before long, tobacco grew into a major industry. As demand in-

creased during the early 1600s, despite the opposition
of King James I, plantations were set up in the British
colony of Virginia. Here, the climate was ideal for
tobacco culture but wood smoke was often used to
assist curing, the leaves being slowly dried without any
undue heating. The result of all such slow methods
of curing was a dull brown tobacco very much like
that still used in cigars and pipes today. According to
tradition, sometime in the 1830s the man in charge
of a curing shed on a plantation in Virginia or North
Carolina—there are various versions of the tale—ran
out of wood for the fire and used charcoal instead. Because of the greater heat and absence of smoke, the
cured tobacco turned out unexpectedly to be a beautiful
golden yellow and smoked with a milder flavour than
the traditional dull brown leaf. This accidental dis-
covery was soon followed by other developments.

Soldiers returning from the Crimean War brought
the cigarette habit back to Britain. In America, advertising and mass production of cigarettes, usually containing the new golden tobacco, increased rapidly
during the second half of the nineteenth century. By
the end of it, cigarettes much like those smoked today
had crossed the Atlantic, largely replacing the Balkan
and Turkish varieties in Europe. The tobacco was
pleasantly mild, cigarettes were convenient, and the
habit could be indulged even in the company of ladies,
for the fumes were much less obnoxious than those
of pipe or cigar. The stage was set for a vast expansion
in cigarette-smoking in which Britain led the world.

By 1930 consumption in England and Wales had
reached nearly 1,400 cigarettes per year for every per-

son aged fifteen or over. In the succeeding years, we led the world again—in deaths from lung cancer and chronic bronchitis. Between 1920 and 1967 the annual toll from lung cancer alone increased by well over fifty times to reach an annual total of more than 28,000, and the figures still appear to be rising remorselessly. Cigarette consumption has risen too and is now running at much more than double the level of thirty years ago. What this will mean in terms of deaths from cigarette-smoking during the next twenty years or so can only be guessed.

Recent research suggests that it may be the method of curing which makes cigarettes so much more hazardous to health than other forms of tobacco. Dull brown tobacco is still cured slowly, if not actually in the open air. During this gradual process, the natural sugars present in tobacco are broken down into harmless compounds by enzymes present in the leaves. Cigarette tobacco, by contrast, acquires its characteristic colour and flavour by more rapid curing at a high temperature which destroys the enzymes. Thus the sugars persist until they are burned in a cigarette and released into the smoke as minute quantities of innumerable different chemical substances. One or more of these appears to be the irritant responsible for the major dangers of cigarette smoking, a big price to pay for golden yellow tobacco with a mild flavour. Though the irritant itself has not yet been isolated, when it has been manufacturers may be able to make ordinary cigarettes free of health hazards. In the meanwhile, the lesson is clear. If you must smoke, keep to pipes and cigars, or to cigarettes made from mild cigar tobacco. Apart from differences in the smoke, they seem to be less habit-forming, and consumption should be lower.

As with other addictions, the motives which lead people to start smoking in the first place are different from those for continuing the habit. Tobacco-smoking also differs from drug abuse proper in that novices seldom expect to experience any change of mood. Most teenagers want to smoke simply to feel grown-up. Other factors may also play a part: curiosity, a desire to conform with the behaviour of their fellows, fear of ridicule for not doing so, or the attraction of something that is frowned on by authority and therefore desirable. Most important of all, though, is the fact that for many teenagers smoking marks the end of childhood.

Once established, the habit may be continued because of a sub-conscious realization that tobacco has a mildly euphoriant, stimulating or even soothing effect on mood. Many people find that offering a cigarette provides a means of breaking the ice with strangers so that smoking has become almost a form of social converse. The whole ritual rigmarole of selecting, lighting, handling and smoking a cigarette has acquired an importance in its own right. The flavour of a particular type of tobacco may be to the smoker's taste, and it has been suggested that the popularity of Virginia tobaccos can be attributed to their greater addictive power. But for many people cigarettes simply gratify the childish, even infantile, need to put something in the mouth. The nervous chain-smoker comforted by drawing on a cigarette has much in common with a baby sucking from a bottle. Smoking provides a socially acceptable alternative to thumb-sucking, nail-biting, pencil-chewing or compulsive sweet-eating.

Whatever their actual reasons for smoking, many people find a tobacco habit hard to break. Even among patients convinced by their doctors of the need to give up cigarettes, only a minority succeed in doing so. Anti-smoking clinics have been singularly unsuccessful, except with those who would probably have managed to break the habit without their help. Anti-smoking tablets containing lobeline, a compound related to nicotine, have been given in the hope of reducing the craving for tobacco, and some success has been reported with hypnosis, but giving up the habit requires more strength of will than most smokers possess. As with all other addictions, prevention is more likely to succeed than attempts at cure—and this is where parents come in.

What parents can do

While teenagers may not be confronted by other drugs, they must be adequately prepared for entry into a smoking, drinking and tablet-taking world. Often this presents no great problem, for children acquire a knowledge of accepted custom as they grow up; but there are two exceptions. Teenagers whose parents are complete abstainers will need instruction, particularly about drinking, if they are not to be launched into the world as complete innocents. Secondly, parents who over-indulge themselves may give a false impression of what is normal, and need to explain that their own example is not a good one. Excessive smoking might be put down to starting the habit before the risk became known, or dependence on tablets to some past period of stress, but for an alcoholic the problem may be almost insuperable. No amount of explanation can make up for an unstable home.

As regards cigarette smoking, since many people find it hard to moderate their habit, and even harder to break it, the ideal is not to start at all. It may help to portray smoking as childish rather than adult; not attractively wicked, but just an extremely expensive way to gamble with your health. However, in the present state of knowledge, pipes, cigars, or the newer brown cigarettes containing cigar tobacco appear to offer a rather safer alternative. A 'with-it' image for the latter among teenagers *might* eventually save thousands of lives a year.

Paradoxically, the chances of becoming an alcoholic appear to be reduced by starting to drink early, in strict moderation and within the family circle. This is what happens in Jewish communities in which both alcoholism and drunkenness are comparatively rare. Alcohol in moderation seems to be much less habit-forming than cigarettes, and early introduction to it allows a child to acquire experience of its use. Of course, this may not prevent a few excesses in the late teens and twenties, but these, too, are part of the learning process. A thumping hangover can be a very salutary lesson.

While drunkenness is unlikely to be missed, the early signs of alcoholism may be subtle. They include:

Unreliable, secretive or aggressive behaviour

Resentment of parental advice or interference

Job changing, dishonesty, shortage of cash or absenteeism

Repeated hangovers, headaches or stomach upsets

Evidence of drinking for other than social reasons (for relief of anxiety, tension or frustration; at unusual hours, especially early in the day; drinking alone and trying to conceal the fact)

Alcoholics usually deny excessive drinking or pass it off with feeble excuses when challenged, and are subject to

Repeated traffic accidents, charges for drunkenness or other offences.

If suggestive signs of this sort are detected the first step is to persuade the budding alcoholic that he has a problem and needs help. Criticism or suggestions that he should pull himself together are inclined to increase frustration and make matters worse. Help can be obtained from Alcoholics Anonymous (whose telephone number is in most town directories), from general practitioners and through them from the psychiatric services, from various religious and voluntary organizations, and from special centres in London, Birmingham and some other towns.

As regards sedative and other drugs, teenagers are increasingly attending general practitioners for sleeplessness, anxiety, 'nerves' or depression. Undoubtedly many of them need help with their problems, but receive tranquillizers, sleeping-tablets or even amphetamines. Thus the underlying problem remains, while the teenager comes to rely on chemical solutions to what may be quite minor difficulties. Though short-term treatment to tide over a crisis may be beneficial, long-term reliance on drugs is no way to train an adolescent for coping with life.

6   The teenage addict—Why?

Why should drug-taking have sprung up so rapidly in Britain during recent years? Why should it particularly involve young people in towns? There are no certain answers to such questions, for little research has been done into the underlying causes of drug abuse and there are consequently few hard facts to go on. Nevertheless, a speculative attempt will be made in this chapter to look at some of the features of modern life that might cause a normal, healthy baby to grow up into a susceptible teenager or even an established heroin addict.

Normal development can be regarded as a gradual transition from the complete dependence of the new-born baby on its mother to the independence of adulthood. Susceptibility to drug dependence appears to be due to failure of this process. Many habitual drug-takers have shallow, immature, unstable personalities and find difficulty in coping with independent existence.

Independence can be enjoyed only on society's terms—by conforming with accepted custom, making satisfactory relationships with other people, behaving in a reasonably sociable fashion, working to earn a living, and keeping on the right side of the law. Independence, in fact, is hedged about with all sorts of social lets and hindrances. The learning and eventual acceptance of these—a process sometimes referred to as 'socialization'—is an essential condition of acceptance as a fully independent member of society. Here, too, there seems to be a failure of development on the part of the susceptible teenager. Unable to relate adequately to society, he cannot find a satisfactory niche in life and is open to the spurious attractions of a delinquent or drug-taking group. Unable to attain full independence, he resents his inability to do so and may break with the unsatisfactory home in which he dimly recognizes the cause of his troubles, so as to prove his manhood. Yet manhood is precisely what he lacks. Dependence on an inadequate home may merely be exchanged for another kind of dependence—on drugs.

According to this view, many susceptible teenagers are immature individuals whose emotional development has not kept pace with physical growth. This is to be expected in the early teens, when the rapid physical development that accompanies puberty normally outstrips the evolution of a mature personality. Thus young teenagers may be highly susceptible to an offer of drugs and are particularly in need of

146

protection. During the teens emotional development should gradually catch up, though it quite often runs behind schedule, leaving the older teenager emotionally immature for his age. This danger period may last only a year or two, but in some cases emotional development is delayed much longer or even diverted on to the wrong lines altogether, producing a seriously disordered (psychopathic) personality. Heroin addicts are not uncommonly of the latter type.

The development of a stable personality depends firstly on inheritance, but as this cannot yet be influenced—except unfavourably—we must confine ourselves to the influence of environment, beginning with the basic requirements for normal emotional development and then looking at some of the features of modern life which affect it adversely.

No period is more crucial to the development of a stable personality than the first few years of life. The baby lying in a cot, totally dependent on its mother for every need and protected by her love, acquires a secure mental foundation, the firm basis on which everything later can be built, the stable homeland of the mind from which the growing child will venture out into the world. Even at this early and vitally important stage of development things can start to go wrong.

An unloved, unwanted or neglected child who has never experienced the security of personal love may have his psychological growth towards independence permanently delayed. Having never experienced the security of true independence, he remains uncertain about the world and consequently lacks the confidence to progress. Thus it is that a bad home begins to create the immature teenager in the first few months of life. Immaturity can be remarkably hard to recognize when enclosed in the body of an apparently tough teenage delinquent taking amphetamines in a coffee bar, but it often has its roots in deprivation of a mother's love.

However, stunting of early emotional development is by no means confined to the classical type of bad home. A 'good' home can sometimes fail, because affluence, intelligence, good management and a whole shelf-full of books on infant care are no substitute for maternal love. Conversely, a devoted mother can sometimes isolate her baby from the effects of rows, divorce, alcoholism or delinquency so that even a slum becomes a good home for the child, at least for the first year or two of life.

Lack of love is not the only danger to a baby's psychological well-being; some are smothered by too much. Over-protected by an over-possessive mother, they remain immature because they are not exposed to even the slightest threat from the environment and have no opportunity to learn for themselves. The mother who always rushes to the loved one at the first whimper when he is only a few days old often goes on to spoil him in other ways. Sometimes she can be clearly recognized sixteen years later. The loved ones may now be pregnant, in trouble with the police or taking drugs: 'I can't understand why it happened. We always gave them everything they wanted.' Many parents have genuinely believed that they were doing their enlightened best for their children by always giving in to them, and are all the more disillusioned when they go wrong. This is an unfortunate legacy

148

of the free expression and over-indulgence that many psychologists were preaching between the wars—and some still are.

There are difficulties of a different kind for the conscientious mother whose anxiety to do the right thing transfers itself to her child. No mental state is more infectious than anxiety and nothing more damaging to the sense of security that a baby needs, and an over-anxious mother may be striving to provide. Anxiety about the details of early upbringing seems widespread among mothers today—perhaps because they are confused by a surfeit of conflicting advice about infant care. Most babies will survive mismanagement of other kinds provided that they are securely wrapped in a cocoon of love, neither fearful of the world outside nor totally isolated from it.

As the toddler first ventures out of the cocoon to explore the outside world, parents begin to encounter the dilemma between freedom and discipline. Should children be brought up with Victorian rigidity or allowed to do whatever they want to without restriction? Many parents who instinctively feel that discipline is an essential feature of upbringing have become confused and irresolute in an age which seems to value permissiveness and free expression more highly. The resulting situation is extremely unsatisfactory. Repressive discipline may be unduly restricting to children, with the result that some grow into frustrated, neurotic adults; too much freedom may be a poor preparation for living in the real world; but uncertainty is worse than either. When discipline alternates illogically with permissiveness in an atmosphere of parental uncertainty, the growing child is deprived of stability, admiration for his parents, and the opportunity to learn where the boundary between freedom and discipline lies. The foundations of a stable personality are undermined.

In such circumstances, which are all too common nowadays, the parents fail to provide a model which children can respect and later copy. A child who has learned that his parents need not be obeyed will first tempt them to punish him by deliberate disobedience, and later despise them for their weakness. The whole situation can deteriorate into a running battle; the child striving to be prematurely free, the parents struggling to maintain some semblance of authority. Such battles are not won. All concerned in them are losers. Family strife, delinquency and drug-taking are just a few of the fruits of defeat.

Ideally, there should be no conflict between freedom and discipline. They are complementary features of a good upbringing, discipline being the condition on which freedom can be enjoyed. The true situation may be pictured as a circular area of freedom surrounded by a protective fence marked discipline. So long as the child remains within the fence he can be completely free, protected both from outside attack and from venturing too far from the safety of home. Thus discipline is not the opposite of freedom, but the protective force without which there could be no freedom at all.

For the first year or two of life, the fence is tightly drawn about the infant. Yet it is not a restrictive barrier, but a protective wall of loving understanding which only a mother or an *individual* mother-substitute can fully penetrate to enter the inner sanctum of the infant's private world. Once confidence is thus established, the fence can move slowly outwards, allowing greater freedom within its walls. More people are admitted to the circle—first the father and other members of the family, then family friends, children of the same age, companions at school or play, and eventually the whole range of contacts presented by the outside world. Step by step the growing child should have the opportunity to learn how fruitful relationships are made with each. At the same time the range of behaviour permitted in the circle increases steadily, new opportunities and interests are added, and the fence imperceptibly changes its character. The firm base of maternal love remains always at the centre, but in childhood the fence must be more authoritarian for a while so that discipline can be learned. At this stage the difficult question of punishment arises.

Naturally, children make mistakes for lack of experience. Naturally, they break rules out of devilment or curiosity. By being caught and reprimanded they learn where the boundaries of their freedom lie. Punishment should not be confused with retribution, nor allowed to disturb the relationship between parent and child, for its proper function is simply to teach the child that transgressing the fence of discipline is not worthwhile. The difficulty for parents is not whether to be firm but where to place the fence at any particular stage of development. This will depend largely on individual convictions and circumstances, but children should obviously have as large an area of freedom as is safely possible so that its boundaries can be seen to be reasonable and fair. If they know where these boundaries are, and are caught crossing them, they will expect to be told off. Parents who are permissive in such circumstances incur contempt for themselves and confuse their children. The main thing is that they should act in accordance with their convictions and avoid vacillating uncertainty. A firm upbringing that is fair and consistent does not destroy love; it may even increase it by showing children that parents really care about their well-being.

Many of the rules of behaviour are learned without invoking the concepts of discipline and punishment at all. They do not even need to be formally taught, for the best method of learning such things—indeed of learning most things in life—is by personal experience, not formal instruction. Human beings are curiously reluctant to learn from the experience of others. Fortunately, we are imbued with sufficient curiosity—especially in childhood—to compensate for this deficiency. We are always prepared to find out for ourselves by trial and error. In many ways the most valuable learning experience that parents can give their children is to make use of this fact by providing as wide a range of different opportunities as possible. But this is not the same thing as giving them everything they want. The growing child needs active involvement in solving the practical problems presented by all kinds of tasks, games and personal relationships with others. Thus his interests are stimulated and his aptitudes developed, but he also learns what will and will not work in practice. Even a toddler playing with simple wooden bricks soon discovers for himself that only certain types of building can be made with them, and an older child soon realizes the necessity for riding his bicycle on the left of the road. The boundary between freedom and discipline is then seen to be in part a natural one— not just an invention of restrictive parents.

By early adolescence the need for imposed discipline and punishment should be fading. As the area of freedom increases further, *self*-discipline and the law increasingly take over the duties at the boundary fence —provided, and only provided, that the earlier stages on the road to independence have been satisfactorily accomplished. Everything depends on that. If parents have not succeeded in implanting love and teaching discipline earlier, they will have no hope of doing so when faced with the natural ebullience, sexuality and sheer force of adolescence. As an American psychiatrist has put it, the adolescent needs to get his parents off his psychic back. And this applies most of all to the immature teenager, unloved or over-protected at home, who must show his independence in order to prove his manhood to himself. By contrast, the more mature teenager, whose parents have encouraged and helped him towards independence, will often feel much less urgent need of it. Adolescence is the age of reckoning when parents discover whether all their earlier efforts have been in vain or not.

It is hoped that the reader will by now be convinced of the basic contention that difficulties in adolescence can almost always be traced back to earlier events, and will have some idea what those events might be. Of course, the situation is never wholly under parental control. Some children inherit much less satisfactory personalities than others and a few will be destined for psychiatric disorder however well they are brought up. Moreover, children cannot be isolated from fashionable attitudes on child-rearing to which they will be exposed at school and elsewhere. If these attitudes are permissive, as they have been in recent years, those who try a strictly disciplinarian approach are almost certain to have a rebellion on their hands when adolescence is reached—if not before.

Even the most carefully planned regimen based on all the right principles is bound to have ups and downs, for it is much easier to write about child-rearing than put it into practice. Nevertheless, the child brought up in a stable home on a basis of secure maternal love and later exposed to a reasonable balance between freedom and opportunity on one hand and discipline on the other, will have been given the only known protection against becoming a teenage delinquent, drug-taker or other social misfit. So long as this basic pattern is followed, a few upsets or mistakes on the way should not hinder development; they may actually help it by providing valuable experience. But the time-table is crowded. Few individuals develop a mature character before their late teens; any major hold-up can defer maturation and thus increase susceptibility to drug dependence.

It may be noted that nothing has been said about intelligence. This is because the immature, dependent or psychopathic teenager may be clever, dull or just plain average; academic distinction is no guarantee of stable personality, and dullness should not be equated with instability of character. The two sets of qualities bear little direct relationship to one another.

To return to the question with which this chapter opened, it must now be obvious that studying the teenager alone will not enable us to say why drug abuse in adolescence has become more common. Its causes appear to lie mainly in influences which weaken family life and undermine the confidence of parents, and thus in the environment to which children are nowadays exposed. No one can say with any certainty which particular factors are the most important, but virtually all can be grouped under the single heading of changes in society. Historically, outbursts of youth unrest have always coincided with periods of social change, and this century can claim to have seen some of the most rapid and fundamental social upheavals experienced by man, followed by widespread evidence of dissatisfaction among young people. It seems reasonable to regard these as cause and effect, and the rise in drug abuse as part of that effect.

Youthful dissatisfaction with the world and its ways has taken two main forms: active protest, whether in the form of delinquency, anti-war demonstrations or just dressing and behaving in an unconventional manner, and passive dropping out into the unreal worlds of mental disorder or drug abuse. Confronted with such clear-cut evidence of its own bankruptcy, the adult world has reacted like a bad parent—looking askance at teenagers to see what is the matter with *them*. Yet the present generation must have the same inherited qualities as its predecessors. If its members behave differently, this can only be because they have been exposed to a different environment during child-hood and adolescence, an environment created not by teenagers themselves but by the adult world.

Protesters, delinquents, hippies, drop-outs and the rest are treated as though society were half afraid of them and more than a little puzzled by their behaviour. The adult world's inability to cope adequately with these problems has led to indecisive and defensive attitudes towards young people, with the result that even strictly neutral words like adolescent and teenager have become unfavourably coloured. For many people adolescents have become a kind of collective enemy, to be viewed with suspicion across a mythical no man's land known as the 'generation gap'. It seems not to have occurred to many adults that they themselves might be the real enemy, the perpetrators of inadequate upbringing, and the creators of an increasingly materialistic and unhappy society. If teenagers cannot cope with life in it, the fault is likely to be ours. Either we have made life too complex and difficult, or pre-pared them badly for it, or both.

Teenagers can be regarded as newcomers viewing the world with fresh and unbiased eyes. If they find much in it to protest about or escape from, we should not blame them for doing so but be glad of the oppor-tunity for seeing ourselves as others see us. If the protest is immature and ill-directed, we should not blame them for that either. It would be absurd to expect an innocent, unjaundiced eye to be coupled with experience. Teenage protest is a sensitive indicator of social ills—probably the most sensitive we have—but not necessarily a guide to the precise nature of

156

those ills, and certainly not a guide to their solution. Both diagnosis and treatment must be the responsibility of experienced adults.

Sadly, instead of responding to protest in a constructive way, society fears and resents it. Thus the generation gap, which is in reality so slight that nobody ever notices crossing it, has become a barrier preventing effective communication. For youthful protestations to have any hope of a hearing they have to go to outrageous and even violent extremes. Even then they are more likely to be rejected out of hand than to stimulate reform. Adults who should know better, not the young protesters, are to blame for this impasse. A rapidly changing society is bound to take wrong turnings at times, and there is as great a need for an early warning system in social affairs as there ever has been against rocket attack. Might not young people provide the sensitive indicators in such a system, showing the approximate areas where trouble lies? And might not this trouble then be seen to be more in society than in the young people pointing it out? As Martin Luther King said, you don't blame the doctor for pointing out the illness.

At present, even anti-war demonstrators who make a reasonably coherent protest are regarded as a bunch of vocal agitators with no respect for law and order. No doubt this is true of a minority, but many are certainly sincere young people with an important message to deliver. Yet society brushes their protestations aside and completely fails to heed the warning signals that something is seriously amiss. Most people do not regard drug-taking as an indicator of underlying

157

social malaise at all, but just as a disease in itself—a disease for which drug pedlars, a few other unsavoury characters and the decadence of modern youth can be held responsible. The addict's 'warning' that he does not much like society, has not been adequately prepared for it, and therefore cannot cope, is almost totally ignored.

If the recent increase in drug abuse among young people is viewed in this sort of light, we must conclude that it is due to changes in society, not in the inherited characteristics of young people. The remainder of this chapter will therefore be devoted to some of the many social changes of recent years that could increase susceptibility to drug abuse. Though such changes do not *cause* addiction, they prepare the soil in which it can take root.

What social changes have affected the newborn babe? It is easy to imagine that the answer should be 'none', that babies bask in the comfort of maternal love as much today as they have ever done. Sadly this is not so. Confinements take place increasingly in hospitals, where babies are all too often accommodated in a separate ward from their mothers. No one considers the psychological well-being of the baby, cast out of the warmth and comfort of the womb into a roomful of squalling infants, who must all suffer the same unhappy fate. No adult could pass a single restful night under such conditions. Some sensitive babies must feel totally rejected, and frightened almost out of their wits. Confused by a multiplicity of nurses and doctors, unable to understand what is happening to them, they are given regular feeds and medical care, but deprived of the security of a mother's love. Is it too much to suggest that this is where some mental ill-health begins?

Breast feeding has become less common. This is not because mothers have less milk than formerly, but because it is inconvenient or 'not quite nice'. Yet bottle-feeding can be an adequate substitute for the breast in the early days of life only when it is accompanied by a similar degree of physical contact, affection and comfort. Confident handling and firm wrapping of a baby are also essential to its sense of security, and probably more important than the precise strength, temperature and timing of its feeds. Can anyone be sure that the feeling of insecurity that results from ignoring such factors has no ill-effect on mental health?

As already briefly mentioned, the anxious mother can transfer her fears to her child. Paradoxically, as life gets physically easier, anxiety seems to increase. In the past, a hard-working mother of ten could be more or less philosophical even if two or three of them died during childhood; nowadays a mild rash or a slight cough often cause maternal consternation and distress. There may be many reasons for this, but there can be no doubt of the damaging effect upon the secure confidence that a young child should have in its mother.

As a child grows older, the emphasis continues to be on physical well-being. Clinics weigh babies, advise about feeding problems and perform immunizations; school medical officers examine new pupils for all manner of diseases. Sometimes even intelligence is assessed, but nobody pays any attention to the development of a stable personality, at least not until it becomes obvious that something is already amiss. Though this situation is hopelessly unbalanced, it could be claimed that matters are no worse than formerly. Not so. In the past, the extended family of assorted grandparents, uncles, aunts and cousins provided both stability and a source of traditional advice. Moreover, society itself was more stable, and young people did not have to be prepared for coping with the competitive and complex world of today.

Separation of a baby from its mother without provision of a personal loving-substitute is perhaps the most serious problem of all. This can arise in the best of families when the mother goes to hospital to have another child; if she goes out to work and leaves the baby at a creche; or if the baby itself has to be admitted to hospital. Such events will do no harm so long as the baby feels secure, but if it feels deprived of mother's love and understanding, this gap cannot be filled by the relatively impersonal provision of material necessities like food, warmth, clothing and somewhere to sleep. In unfavourable circumstances separation of a young baby from its mother can be a shattering experience impeding psychological development. Sometimes the same thing can happen even in the care of the mother if the child feels unwanted, or sees affection being showered on a new baby.

On the other hand, separation is not always harmful. Explanations and reassurance—when a child is old enough to understand them—can turn a short spell of separation into a valuable learning experience; and a personal mother-substitute can be perfectly satis-
160

factory for short periods or long, as the success of adoption clearly shows. Though these things are widely recognized today, the high rates of illegitimacy, divorce, and broken or bad homes continue to put the mental health of thousands of young children in jeopardy.

Lack of a stable and settled home is scarcely less damaging to older children, indeed the earlier damage is often compounded. This may be no commoner than in the past, but what does seem to be commoner is uncertainty among 'good' parents. Undecided about religion, about moral values, about standards of behaviour, many have become absurdly permissive under the influence of social change. Taken by itself permissiveness is purely negative, and too often consists of lack of training, lack of protective love, lack of stability, lack of discipline, lack of opportunity, and lack of responsibility. In recent years, the emphasis in society has been so strongly on freedom and individual rights—even the right to poison yourself with drugs—that it is easy to lose sight of the fact that without responsibility and discipline there can be no freedom.

But society is affluent as well as permissive. Perhaps sensing their failure to provide an adequate upbringing, parents shower their children with material goods. Far from compensating for other deficiencies this makes matters worse. The child is first trained that he can do whatever he likes, and then that he can have whatever he wants, all without any effort on his part. Emotional development towards a stable adult personality may be permanently stunted by this combination of permissiveness and spoiling. Is it any wonder that some young people turn to drugs just at the point when they should be embarking on a career?

What children nowadays lack, and adolescents lack most of all, is not freedom but opportunity—opportunity to do practical things, to play games, to take responsibility, to learn by being actively involved, by making an effort to succeed, and even to learn from failure. Children have much to learn that cannot be taught in school, and will never be absorbed by sitting passively in front of a television set. Being given a ready-made article is no substitute for struggling to make one. Watching a football match is no substitute for playing the game. How many children nowadays play an instrument, instead of perpetually listening to canned music? How many ride a horse instead of watching westerns? How many make their own beds or do the washing-up instead of leaving it to mother? How many read books instead of watching television? How many go for walks and cycle rides in the country instead of travelling into town by bus or car?

Few modern teenagers have ever been physically extended. Walking under a hot sun until exhausted, swimming in a cold river instead of a heated pool, cycling home soaked to the skin, running across country on a cold winter's day—these are all things of the past. Few children today have grown a plant, picked an apple or even podded peas. Fewer still have experienced close contact with animals, let alone seen them breeding, giving birth or dying. Though no one would criticize the reduction in human illness, poverty and early death, many people grow up nowadays without any direct experience of adversity, surely one of the most valuable learning processes in the building of a mature personality. In all these fields second-hand experience, usually via the television screen, has taken the place of the real thing. Should we be surprised if some teenagers find they cannot cope with the real world and want to escape from it into a new one of their own making? Should we blame them if the new one they choose is synthetic too?

The weakening of family life, decline of organized religion and break-up of conventional patterns of behaviour make society seem much less moral than in the past, because the case for morality often goes by default. Immorality gets such a good press that it is difficult for young people to develop a firm conviction that drug abuse or pre-marital intercourse—to take but two common examples—are undesirable. Ridiculous over-simplifications are used, sometimes by well-known people, to make marihuana seem harmless and the law stupid for continuing to ban it. Progressive psychiatrists who should know better naïvely tell the world that young people no longer have any problems with sex because they simply do what they want to. Venereal disease and the frequently damaging effect of promiscuity on the later mental stability of women are ignored, as though the 'pill' solved every problem. Society is not only permissive and affluent, it sometimes actually encourages immorality. In T. S. Eliot's words, we live in 'an age which advances progressively backwards'.

Much of modern life tends to foster immaturity. There is no need to save up for a rainy day, because the State will provide when you are ill, unemployed or old. There is no need for long hours of hard physical labour because machines have taken over and rates of pay are high—especially for teenagers. In such a society the father ceases to be the strong head of the family, the provider and protector. Often he is reduced to a subordinate role in which his only masculine attributes are smoking, drinking and driving the car, while the mother really runs the household. Robbed of his masculine role, the father loses authority with his children and fails to provide the strong pattern on which teenagers should model themselves. Instead, they remain dependent, child-like, on the mother. Thus social security, high wages and better living conditions, the very things that are supposed to strengthen society, often weaken its most essential element—the family—and hinder the development of a mature, independent personality.

Other social changes have had a similar effect. Technological progress has made instant solutions possible in many fields, so that adults now enjoy the same immediate gratification of desires as a child. If we want to go somewhere we jump in a car or plane. If we want to speak to someone we pick up the telephone. If we want entertainment we switch on the television. If we want to acquire something we buy it ready-made. No effort is required. Money can often be earned without hard work. Sexual desire can be gratified without the tiresome preliminaries of courtship and marriage. Even abortion is available almost on demand. There is a pill for every ailment, an instant effortless solution to every problem. But there is no longer any cause to serve, no God but personal satisfaction. Adversity, pain, endeavour, healthy exhaustion, the long hard struggle against the odds are gone. With them have gone the joy of achievement and the stimulus of failure. In their place, in this push-button age, are the relatively child-like qualities of gratification and frustration. Is it surprising that some young people never progress beyond this stage? Should we criticize the idealistic few who protest that life should hold something better?

As life becomes increasingly complex, the body is less physically exerted, but the brain is constantly under stress. Frustrations increase, and with them come unhappiness, headaches, sleeplessness, anxiety, depression, neurosis, all the ills of so-called civilization; to be relieved by yet more instant solutions. Teenagers who take drugs to change their mood or escape from reality are mimicking in exaggerated form the accepted behaviour of adults who over-indulge in tobacco, alcohol, tranquillizers or other medications.

Nowadays, even recreation usually consists more of mental than physical activities. Instead of restoring a balance by taking physical exercise, most people relax in front of the television, and allow their brains to be assaulted by a surfeit of synthetic experience, a sort of passive mental gymnastics to drive out the frustrations of the day. The same imbalance between mental and physical activity is becoming established in schools and universities. Sport is steadily being pushed out by the demands of examinations. Worse still, the increasing load of mental work consists largely of a purely academic exercise, the accumulation of facts. This can be both a poor preparation for problem-solving in the real world and yet another hindrance to the development of a mature personality. The teenager exposed to such teaching—it is hardly education—has little time or energy left for sport or other activities. He relaxes, when the pressure of homework permits, either in front of the television like his parents or being deafened by pop music. It is noteworthy that the first generation to be reared on television in this country is also the one that turned to dependence on pop, and sometimes drugs as well.

Neither television nor pop music need be harmful in itself, but when used to excess they prevent conversation, inhibit social life and deprive children of the opportunity to take part in active pursuits or make friends. One American survey has shown that many schoolchildren actually spend more time each year watching television than they do in class. Some teenagers become so dependent on electronic stimulation that they begin to live only when 'turned on' by pop. Particularly for those doing dull factory jobs, it affords their only release from the mixture of boredom and meaningless activity that fills their lives. For others this is just a passing phase, but some of the most immature become 'hooked'—only to find that electronic addiction gradually loses its effect. When deafening noise will no longer drive all sense out of their heads and transport them to another world, they begin to look for other emotional kicks. If pop music won't 'turn them on', drugs will.

In America it is fashionable to attribute the increase in drug abuse among hippies and others to such grave problems as the Vietnam war, social and racial inequality, the armaments race and the ever-present threat of nuclear warfare. These are said to operate by stimulating both protest and a desire to escape from a society that preaches peace and equal opportunity but practises the opposite. How important such feelings may be it is hard to say. Disillusionment with the adult world is certainly widespread among teenagers, but there is little evidence that world or even national events are a major cause of drug abuse in Britain.

Finally, of course, there are the predisposing factors already outlined in the first chapter: more young teenagers living alone in towns with more time on their hands than ever in the past; many of them susceptible individuals who have left a bad home, and all liable to encounter an offer of habit-forming drugs from friends, addicts or pushers.

To sum up, there is no single cause of teenage drug-taking. Many facets of modern life tend to hinder the development of a mature personality. By contrast, physical maturity is attained at an increasingly early age as a result of better housing, feeding and medical care. Thus the fourteen- or fifteen-year-old may find himself trying to control the surging physical and sexual forces of an adolescent body with the mind of a child. A long period of potential frustration ensues. Whether the teenager does a dull, repetitive factory job or goes on from school to university, he is as likely to be bored or frustrated as to be given opportunities to develop his personality and use his talents. Teenagers today are better taught and physically fitter than their predecessors. They have more money, more leisure and more freedom, but opportunities for active involvement in society are lacking; the adult world provides few outlets for the impulses, emotions, abilities, intelligence, physical strength, idealism and imagination of youth. Instead of making use of these qualities—which are sorely needed and in short supply —it stifles them. As Dr Margaret Lowenfeld has said, if the force of adolescence is not made use of, it explodes. Are the teenagers the sole culprits if the force that is in them explodes into protest marches, hippyism, promiscuity, delinquency, dangerous driving, violence and drug abuse?

With so many adverse factors at work, it may seem surprising that most adolescents still do not take drugs. But there is little room for complacency on this account. The social changes which seem to be the cause of increased drug-taking are relatively recent; we cannot afford to sit back and assume that the whole thing will prove to be just another passing fashion.

In the modern world there is more to be fitted into the fixed interval between birth and adulthood than was the case in more settled times. To keep their footing in the swirling currents of social change, young people today need a firmer foundation than their predecessors, but they seldom get it. To cope with the increasing complexity of life, they need more opportunities to learn by practical experience from an early age, but they do not get them.

7 What has been and could be done

Ideas on the prevention and treatment of addiction vary widely even among the experts. What might be done to prevent and treat it in the future may be more readily understood against a background of past events. For many years there was a sharp contrast between the liberal approach in this country, where addicts were generally regarded as patients in need of treatment, and the USA, where they were punished as criminals. Though the situation in both countries has now changed somewhat, these two systems typify the main attitudes towards addiction: it is treated either as a crime or an illness.

Under the British system, people addicted to the hard drugs were able to obtain supplies from a general practitioner on certain conditions. These were defined by the Rolleston Committee in 1926 and covered 'Persons for whom, *after every effort has been made for the cure of addiction*, the drug cannot be completely withdrawn'. The section in italics was never strictly enforced. Though not formally registered with the doctor or with the authorities, the names of addicts became known to the Home Office through records kept by chemists, and they were commonly referred to as 'registered'. Until 1960 they numbered about 450. The great majority were aged over fifty, slightly more than half were women, and most had first received dangerous drugs as medical treatment. Such patients are known as 'therapeutic addicts', and they are usually addicted to the less potent hard drugs like pethidine or methadone in tablet form, rather than heroin or morphine by injection. Dosage tends to remain unchanged, and therapeutic addicts differ in many other respects from young heroin-takers. As might be expected among middle-aged and elderly people, many of whom suffer from chronic diseases, crime is infrequent and recruitment of newcomers minimal. In many cases their condition is such that doctors can prescribe for them in good conscience, knowing that treatment enables them to live a normal life, instead of making it impossible.

Apart from therapeutic addicts, some doctors and nurses became addicted to drugs to which they had access in their work, but the numbers in both groups have been steady for many years, and there is no reason to regard them as a major social problem. Before 1960, there were comparatively few young adults addicted to heroin or morphine, and in most years no teenage addicts at all. For these and other reasons, the British system was viewed with envy from across the Atlantic where things were very different.

After the American Civil War, with its innumerable therapeutic addicts created by morphine treatment, hard drugs continued to be freely available and addiction widespread until well into the present century. Faced with this situation and the need to comply with its international obligations (under the Hague Convention of 1912) for controlling traffic in narcotics, the U.S. Government enacted the Harrison Narcotic Act in 1914, and other harsh legislation followed. These laws had three main effects. Unauthorized possession of narcotics became a serious offence, doctors were forbidden to prescribe for addicts, and heroin was banned altogether. Offenders received stiff sentences and addicts sent to gaol suffered the full horrors of the withdrawal syndrome without treatment. As a result, traffic in hard drugs was driven underground, and a multi-million dollar black market, believed to be controlled by the Mafia, thrived in the underworld of many American cities. To pay for their own drugs, existing addicts had to resort to crime or create new addicts by introducing others—usually youngsters because they were the most susceptible—to a drug habit and then selling them supplies.

Thus the measures which were supposed to combat hard drug abuse in the States not only failed to control its spread but actually opened the door to the black market and fostered close links between addiction and crime. Treatment facilities were almost non-existent, and imprisonment resulted in no more than a temporary cure while the addict was in gaol—followed by an almost invariable return to drug-taking when he went back to his old environment. In the 'twenties, when there were thought to be several hundred thousand narcotic addicts, centres were set up for their treatment, but these proved unsuccessful and were closed after a few years. Though political influences seem to have played a part in this decision, underlying the closure was the feeling that treatment consisted not so much of curing addicts as giving them drugs.

Yet if treatment centres do not provide supplies there is no incentive for addicts to attend them. This is the great dilemma. Either the addict is given drugs, in which case he will continue to attend only as long as his demands are met, or he is refused legal supplies and turns instead to the black market. In either case he is likely to remain an addict, and the percentage of cures is unlikely to rise above single figures. It is easy to see why many American experts envied the British system, but by no means certain that the low addiction rates and absence of trafficking in hard drugs before 1960 were actually due to the system. We may merely have been able to afford a liberal attitude because there were so few addicts.

When the number of addicts in Britain began to rise during the early sixties, it was due to a minor breakdown in the system, not the activities of criminal pushers. The rapid increase among those under 35 and especially in their teens and twenties can be seen from the table, though the true totals were probably twice as great.

These figures cover all dangerous drugs and conceal the fact that less than 10 per cent of addicts over 50 take heroin, compared with 90 per cent or more of young addicts.

Dangerous ('hard') Drug Addicts Known to the Home Office:

Age:	14-15	16-17	18-19	20-34	35-49	over 50	Total
1959				50	92	278	454
1960			1	62	91	267	437
1961			2	94	95	272	470
1962		1	2	132	107	274	532
1963		4	13	184	128	298	635
1964	1	9	30	257	138	311	753
1965	8	24	113	347	134	291	927
1966	18	94	217	558	162	286	1349
1967	3	120	272	906	142	279	1729

1968 (*provisional notifications to 12th December*) 2479

It particularly is noteworthy that there has been no increase in the number of older addicts, among whom women continue to predominate. By contrast, approximately three-quarters of the new young addicts were male, the rising trend first becoming apparent in the 20-34 age group, in which the figures nearly doubled from 50 in 1959 to 94 in 1961. This information would have been available by the end of 1961, but it was not until July 1964, when the number had climbed into the two hundreds and many teenagers were involved, that the Minister of Health belatedly took action. He appointed a committee. Or, more accurately, he asked the Inter-departmental Committee (known as the Brain Committee, after its chairman) to reconsider 'the advice they gave in 1961 in relation to the prescribing of addictive drugs by doctors'.

The Brain Committee's 1961 report had reassuringly stated that since the number of addicts was small and static, the position was satisfactory and no major changes were required. With benefit of hindsight, it is now possible to see that the committee's advice might have been different if they had looked more closely at the increase (24 per cent in one year) among young addicts. The apparently static total figures published in the first report conceal the early signs of a trend towards the young heroin addict, which was already under way when the report was issued in 1961.

When the Brain Committee reported again in 1965, the evidence was only too plain, and most of its earlier recommendations were reversed. In view of the disturbing increase in addiction to heroin and cocaine, especially among young people, the committee concluded that addicts should be notified to a central authority, that special treatment centres (with some compulsory powers) should be set up, and that only doctors on the staffs of these centres should be permitted to prescribe heroin and cocaine for addicts. Meanwhile, Parliament had enacted the Drugs (Prevention of Misuse) Act 1964 and the Dangerous Drugs Act 1965 to restrict supplies of habit-forming drugs and prohibit their unauthorized possession. The Brain Committee's recommendations of July 1965 had to wait until the Dangerous Drugs Act of August 1967, and were not finally implemented until April 1968 —without compulsory powers for treating addicts. Eight years had elapsed between the initial increase in heroin addiction among young people and this action being taken. In those eight years, a hard core of heroin addiction became established in the community. The number of known heroin addicts under twenty rose from 1 to 395, the number between twenty and thirty-four from 62 to 906. If those not known to the Home Office could be included, the increase would no doubt be larger still.

The 1965 report concludes that

> the major source of supply has been the activity of a very few doctors who have prescribed excessively for addicts. Thus we were informed that in 1962 one doctor alone prescribed almost 600,000 tablets of heroin (i.e. 6 kilogrammes) for addicts. The same doctor, on one occasion, prescribed 900 tablets of heroin to one addict and, three days later, prescribed for the same patient another 600 tablets 'to replace pills lost in an accident'. Further prescriptions of 720 and 840 tablets followed later to the same patient. Two doctors each issued a single prescription for 1,000 tablets. These are only the more startling examples. We heard of other instances of prescriptions for considerable, if less spectacular, quantities of dangerous drugs over a long period of time. Supplies on such a scale can easily provide a surplus that will attract new recruits to the ranks of the addicts.

In all, eighty per cent of the heroin produced in this country in 1962 went to addicts and three-quarters of this was prescribed by one doctor.

The Committee went on to say 'that not more than six doctors have prescribed these very large amounts of dangerous drugs *for individual patients* . . .' (my italics). In other words, these doctors were not just treating large numbers of addicts, they were irresponsibly over-prescribing. The remedy was plain: take action against the six doctors, either in the courts or by the Home Secretary (who already had wide but unused powers) withdrawing their authority to possess, supply or prescribe dangerous drugs. Only a committee could have reached any other conclusion—and the Brain Committee did.

The 'not more than six doctors' mainly responsible for the spread of heroin addiction were excused on the grounds that they had 'acted within the law and according to their professional judgement'. Instead of recommending that action should be taken against them, the committee proposed that the right to prescribe heroin and cocaine for addicts should be withdrawn from all doctors except those in the new centres. Since legislation was required, this meant in effect that nothing was done after the 1965 report for almost three years, during which time the number of addicts in their teens and twenties *trebled*.

It may be that the British system would have failed anyway when confronted by large numbers of addicts. It may be that the law would have had to be changed as a result. But in fact the system itself did not fail; the authorities responsible for its proper working negligently allowed it to be abused by a tiny minority of doctors, until it had to be abandoned. The situation can be roughly compared with allowing half-a-dozen dangerous drivers to run amok on the roads for eight years, causing endless accidents and not a few deaths, without ever bringing them to book—and then making car driving illegal for everybody so as to put a stop to the menace.

When the Brain Committee recommended restricting the right to prescribe for addicts, they were conscious that 'restrictions so severe as to prevent or seriously discourage the addict from obtaining any supplies from legitimate sources' might 'lead to the development of an organized illicit traffic. The absence hitherto of such an organized illicit traffic has been attributed largely to the fact that an addict has been able to obtain supplies of drugs legally.' The committee clearly felt that their new proposals would 'make it more difficult for addicts to obtain supplies of heroin and cocaine', without 'sacrificing the basic advantages of the present arrangements'. In other words, they believed that the essence of the British system was being retained. Addicts could still obtain legal supplies; but they would have to go to special treatment centres to get them. 'At the same time the risk that illicit traffic in drugs will in any event increase has to be accepted.'

Writing at the beginning of 1969, when the treatment centres have been open only a few months, it is impossible to say whether the new policy will reduce the number of addicts. Notifications last year show that more addicts have so far come forward than were previously known to the Home Office, but there is no way of gauging how many are still unknown to the authorities. And it remains to be seen whether heroin addicts, who are notoriously unpredictable, will accept regular attendance at one of the centres established at large hospitals and open only at set hours. Especially if pressure is put on them to reduce dosage, or be admitted for withdrawal of drugs, they may abscond or turn to the black market. There is already some indirect evidence of resistance to the treatment centres. Since they were established, demand for the injectable form of methyl amphetamine has, to quote one report, been 'hundreds of thousands times greater during one quarter of 1968 than the total for any previous year'— and many addicts regard methyl amphetamine as a possible substitute for heroin. As a result of this sinister development supplies of the drug were restricted to hospitals only from the end of September 1968.

Since there is now a standing Advisory Committee on Drug Dependence, action to restrict methyl amphetamine was at least taken within months instead of years. But the very fact that such a dramatic increase in demand coincided with the opening of addiction centres suggests that addicts were turning elsewhere. It also raises once more the question of wholly irresponsible prescribing, for, as *The Lancet* put it, 'this drug has been readily provided on prescription by certain doctors'. They are now said to be rather more than six in number. While such doctors could justify giving heroin to addicts in the past on the pretext that other treatment facilities were inadequate, there can be no possible justification for prescribing methyl amphetamine for injection. The motive was presumably greed. It is high time that effective disciplinary measures should be taken against doctors who corrupt young people for their own ends; but there is also a need for action in a wider field. To quote *The Lancet* again: 'the cutting-off of each newly abused drug is no substitute for greater efforts to uncover and counter the real reasons for drug abuse'.

What greater efforts can be made? The whole addiction problem has been so hedged about with conditions and assumptions that the room left for manoeuvre is negligible. In keeping with current fashion the emphasis is not on responsibilities but rights. The doctor's right to prescribe whatever he thinks fit for his patient is fiercely defended by the medical profession. We hear rather less of the addict's right to poison himself privately with drugs if he wants to, but even this idea is seriously put forward from time to time. Enlightened people insist that drug-taking is not a crime or even a misdemeanour, but a disease, and assume that it must therefore be treated with tea and sympathy. In support of this view it is stated that cutting addicts off from supplies forces them on to the black market—which is probably true—and that compulsory treatment nearly always fails, which need not necessarily be true. The net effect of this series of assumptions is to make the addiction problem virtually insoluble. Only voluntary treatment remains; and voluntary treatment cures only those few addicts with both the desire and the strength of will to break their habit. For treatment to be more effective in the future, something will have to give. If its scope continues to be limited by the conditions imposed at present, efforts to cure the great majority of addicts will almost certainly continue to fail, and their numbers to rise.

It must be obvious that none of the conditions mentioned is absolute. A doctor's freedom to prescribe should certainly be limited if he misuses it, though this need not necessarily mean banning all doctors from prescribing a particular drug. The individual's theoretical right to poison himself in private—if it exists at all—is unacceptable in practice because addicts tend to corrupt others and become a burden on the community themselves. The older group of mainly therapeutic addicts on stable dosage of milder drugs is an exception, but attempts to stabilize heroin addicts in this way have had scant success. By his whole anti-social way of life the heroin addict forfeits any sort of right to his habit. Society must be entitled to protect its own interests, and save the addict from himself, by insisting on compulsory treatment.

Compulsory treatment should not be confused with imprisonment and immediate withdrawal of all drugs, nor does it mean treating addiction as a crime rather than a disease. It merely implies that the need for treatment to protect the individual and the community is great. There are several good precedents for compulsion. Mentally ill patients who represent a serious risk to themselves or others are certified and confined compulsorily in hospital. Powers also exist for compulsory treatment of certain infectious diseases. Yet the heroin addict, whose mental condition and tendency to infect others make him a candidate for inclusion in both these categories, can be treated under the present law only if he wishes to be. This seems scarcely less unreasonable than sentencing addicts to prison and giving them no treatment or after-care. Writing in his journal, *Household Words*, in January 1851, Charles Dickens described two children 'whose heads scarcely reached the top of the dock', who were sentenced to be whipped for stealing a loaf of bread. 'Can the State devise no better sentence for its children?', he asked, 'Will it never sentence them to be taught!' Society has heeded Dickens' plea, but how long will it be before we sentence addicts to be treated?

Voluntary treatment puts the responsibility for his cure on the addict himself, thus imposing a strain that he is ill-fitted to bear. It ignores the widely accepted facts that he is an immature and inadequate person who could not cope with life in the first place, and that heroin has further undermined his ability to do so. To expect such a person to summon up sufficient will-power to break his habit permanently is patently absurd; heroin is much more persuasive than any arguments the doctor can use.

Even the methods of voluntary treatment usually employed seem to ignore the fundamental immaturity of the addict's personality. What he commonly receives is a confusing mixture of sympathetic help and admonishment to cut down dosage, accompanied by supplies of drugs and perhaps group psychotherapy. What he needs—after compulsory withdrawal of all habit-forming drugs—is to experience both the security of a home and the opportunities for active participation in life of which he was very probably deprived in childhood. In this way his personality should gradually mature. When doctors say in effect to heroin addicts, 'Yes, you can have your drugs, but you shouldn't really be taking them, you know', they are echoing the indulgent, confused parents who might have been the cause of the problem in the first place. The addict is left with no clear idea whether he is supposed to give up his habit or not. Moreover, no drug is known which can help to mature personality, and psychiatric treatment is hardly more successful. Present methods of

handling the drug-taker seem more likely to perpetu-
ate immaturity than end it, even when they are accompanied by attempts to rehabilitate him. In some ways
these methods resemble handing out pound notes to
delinquents so as to gain their confidence and prevent
thieving, and then confidently waiting for them to
grow up into responsible citizens.

In recent years, while the old British system has been
largely abandoned in favour of stricter controls, the
emphasis in the United States has been shifting from
punishment towards treatment, including what is
known as civil commitment. This consists of treating
the addict compulsorily in a hospital or rehabilitation
centre. Writing of the need for compulsion, the New
York* authority Dr Donald Louria has pointed out
that neither gaol nor voluntary treatment frequently
effects full rehabilitation of addicts. More often there
is a cycle of treatment or gaol, followed sooner or later
by a return to drugs. 'Yet the addict can be rehabili-
tated; even if early attempts are ineffective, many will
mature out of drug use of their own volition by the
age of thirty-five or forty. The problem is to
rehabilitate addicts while they are still young, before
repeated jail sentences have left an indelible mark, or
overdose or infection kill them.'

Civil commitment can take several different forms.
It may be an alternative to trial or imprisonment, or
the addict's family can initiate commitment even if
he has not been charged with crime. Finally, the addict
can voluntarily sign himself on for treatment which

* *Nightmare Drugs*, by Donald Louria, M.D., Pocket Books Inc.,
New York, 1966.

then becomes compulsory for a fixed period.

Since gradual withdrawal of heroin need never take longer than about three weeks, the initial medical treatment of addiction is relatively simple and quick—so long as the doctor, not the addict, is in charge. At this stage the addict must be confined in hospital and he will very probably be acutely resentful. This need not matter provided that compulsory withdrawal of the drug is followed by prolonged rehabilitation, designed both to mature the former addict's inadequate personality and 'socialize' him as a useful member of the community. The emphasis must be on opportunity— opportunity to learn a job, lead a normal life, make friends, take part in all sorts of activities, and eventually marry, settle down and have a family. Only in one respect need there be any special restriction. In return for society's determination to restore him to normal life, the former addict has to submit to a form of modified probation extending over many years, to ensure that he does not revert to drugs. Frequent blood or urine tests and a suspended prison sentence, which comes into force only if probation is broken, may well be essential to enforce continued abstinence. Such a regime, though resented at first, can even give the ex- addict something else he lacks—a sense of security, a feeling that he matters to someone—until such time as he finally settles down with a family of his own.

Since the first civil commitment programmes (in California and New York) only started in the early sixties, there are as yet no firm figures to prove the superiority of the method. However, preliminary results were sufficiently promising for the U.S. Government to pass the Narcotic Addict Rehabilitation Act of 1966, making civil commitment a national policy. Addicts who opt for civil commitment instead of trial are committed for a three-year period, during which they may not withdraw from treatment, though much of this time would be spent under supervised out-patient care in the community after an initial spell in hospital. Much the same applies to addicts committed by themselves or their relatives, while convicted addicts can be compulsorily treated for up to ten years, the first six months of which is spent in a rehabilitation institution. Despite this compulsion, the emphasis of the new law—as its name implies—is heavily on rehabilitation in the community. Measures include 'vocational training, continuing education, job placement, social casework, individual psychotherapy and group or family therapy. Halfway houses and day or night hospitals may also be used.' Special field offices will operate where there are large concentrations of addicts, and tests be done to determine whether there has been a return to drugs. 'The primary after-care services . . . are those which prevent or relieve family problems, help the patient stabilize his financial status, and develop his ability to earn a living and cope with the stresses of daily life.'

With greater experience of compulsory schemes which are not punitive but provide the addict with the opportunity to help himself, there seems no reason why success rates should not climb steadily. In America the huge numbers of addicts (around 35,000 in New York alone) and the highly organized illicit drug traffic present major obstacles, but in this country—

still without an established black market and with comparatively few addicts—the prospects are brighter.

A really intensive civil commitment programme could get virtually all the known heroin addicts in Britain off the drug within a matter of months. They would then need close supervision to prevent them obtaining illicit supplies, and enthusiastic application of a comprehensive rehabilitation programme. The expense of doing the job properly would be high, probably several million pounds a year for the first few years. But the cost should fall rapidly as the number of addicts dropped and the core of infection was removed from the community.

Is this just a pipe dream? When one looks at the possible alternatives, it seems the only rational course. It is true that voluntary treatment and such organizations as Narcotics Anonymous can help to cure the few addicts firmly resolved to break their habit, but the great majority—probably over ninety per cent—need an external source of resolve in the form of compulsory withdrawal followed by enforced abstinence. This will continue to be true whatever drugs or other forms of treatment are developed for heroin or any other type of addiction; without compulsion they are almost bound to fail. The real alternative to rigorous action does not lie in new methods—but with a rapid increase in the number of addicts. An American research institute has forecast that there will be 11,000 heroin addicts in Britain by 1972 if present trends continue. Unless English addicts prove much more amenable than their transatlantic counterparts, this forecast seems likely to be fulfilled. If so, the core of

infection in the community and the sheer size of the
illicit drug trade might mean that drug abuse in Britain
could become almost ineradicable—by 1972.

Of course, civil commitment of heroin addicts could
at best solve only one aspect of the whole drug abuse
problem, though a rehabilitative probation service,
once started, could be extended to cover soft-drug
takers as well. Illicit importation and peddling of all
habit-forming drugs would need to be rigorously controlled and penalties made fiercer than at present to
act as a deterrent, and especially to protect the young.
More research would be needed into all aspects of
drug abuse. Manufacturers, importers, wholesalers,
chemists and doctors would have to do much more
to prevent drugs getting into the wrong hands. As
suggested in earlier chapters, children would need
proper instruction about drug abuse; both parents and
teachers would need to know how to recognize its
early signs; and some thought should be given to
methods for strengthening the family and combating
the many things in modern life that may make young
people susceptible to a drug habit. Above all, a successful anti-drug abuse campaign would have to be versatile
and wide-awake; constantly on the watch for new
trends and ways to counter them.

All this could be done. Basically, it is simply a
question of society deciding whether it really wants to
be rid of widespread drug abuse among young people,
and whether it is prepared to foot the bill. Every man,
woman and child in the country might have to pay
several shillings a year to do it, though many people
would probably feel that the money was well spent if

it reduced the risk of their own children or grand-children becoming dependent on drugs. But wider problems would remain.

Clearing up drug abuse might be in vain unless more attention were given to the needs of growing children and to the force of adolescence that explodes unless it is made use of. At present no more than a small minority of teenagers are emotionally immature for their age, but the numbers could well increase if upbringing becomes less satisfactory. At present, the proportion of teenagers who opt out because they cannot cope with life is relatively small, but it could also rise as life becomes increasingly complex and impersonal. At present, not many teenagers are so frustrated by lack of opportunities and useful outlets for their energies that they actively protest or react with violence, but their ranks seem to be growing. If the adult world does not heed the warning signs or hear the voice of youth, its dubious standards will persist—until drug abuse becomes more common, or something else comes to pervert the soul.

Appendixes

I   First-aid in cases of overdosage

First-aid for coma due to drug overdosage is essentially the same as for any other unconscious patient. The following routine should therefore be adopted whether unconsciousness is due to sudden illness, attempted suicide, drug abuse or even a simple fainting attack. In practice, it may be impossible to distinguish between them though a person who has fainted will usually recover before there has been time to call an ambulance.

1. Do not panic. Do not throw cold water over the patient. Do not move him unless it is necessary for his own safety (if he has fallen near a fire, for instance). There is unlikely to be any immediate danger to life, provided breathing is maintained.

2. Place the patient face downward on the floor (or a bed) without a pillow in the semi-prone position with the head turned to one side. This prevents choking due to vomiting and stops the tongue falling back-

wards into the throat. On no account should an unconscious person be propped up in a chair or allowed to lie on the back.

3. Remove any false teeth, see that the mouth and throat are clear, and then hold the chin up to ease breathing. Loosen collar and any tight clothing around the abdomen. Try and obtain someone to help.

4. Telephone the emergency services (dial 999), and ask for 'ambulance'. Give your name and address, and explain that you have an unconscious patient, thought to be suffering from an overdose of drugs, who requires urgent removal to hospital. In such cases it is not essential for the patient to be seen by a doctor first.

5. Telephone the doctor to enquire if he is immediately available. Say the ambulance has been called, but do not waste time on repeated calls to other doctors.

6. Check that patient's breathing is still satisfactory, the mouth clear and chin raised. If necessary, keep warm with blankets, but *not* hot water bottles.

7. If the patient can be left, search for tablets, bottles, pill boxes (even empty ones), syringes, ampoules etc., or any other evidence (prescriptions, hospital attendance cards, name and address of doctor) that might help in identifying the drugs taken. Take them to the hospital together with any vomited material. Without such evidence, the doctor may be unable to tell what drug or drugs have been taken, and may not know what treatment is required.

8. If there is still time, telephone the casualty department of the local hospital, and advise them to expect an unconscious patient probably suffering from an overdose of drugs.

9. Wait for the ambulance to arrive. Ensure that patient is placed on a stretcher still in the semi-prone position without pillows and with the head to one side.

Never try to get a sleepy or unconscious patient to drink, or make him sick.

If breathing fails due to drug overdose, mouth-to-mouth or artificial respiration are unlikely to help. But remember that a patient who is not breathing may simply have the throat obstructed by dentures, vomit or the tongue falling back—all of which can be cleared rapidly.

If a patient is still fully conscious after taking an overdose by mouth, make him sick by pushing a spoon handle or finger down the throat. Then give him a drink of strong salt water (about one tablespoon of salt dissolved in a tumbler of warm water) and make him sick again.

II Drugs and the police—What to do if a teenager is involved

Parents may first learn that a teenager has been taking drugs when they hear of his (or her) arrest. If heroin, cocaine, marihuana or related substances are concerned, the police can arrest without warrant anyone suspected of committing—or being about to commit—an offence under the Dangerous Drugs Acts. In the case of amphetamines, hallucinogens and other drugs covered by the Drugs (Prevention of Misuse) Act, a suspect may be arrested without warrant if a constable has reason to believe that he might abscond, cannot obtain his name and address, or is not satisfied that those given are true. Moreover, the police have powers to detain suspects (and/or stop vehicles) to carry out a search. In any such event, the suspect is likely to be taken to a police station and given the usual warning that anything he says may be taken down and used in evidence.

Drugs And Police—If A Teenager Is Involved

In the case of a teenager, the parents would normally be notified at this stage. After going to the police station, and perhaps arranging for a solicitor to attend, their first step should be to establish the nature of the alleged offence and find out whether a charge has been preferred. Though there are a number of possible offences, the charge of unauthorized possession of a drug contrary to one of the above acts is by far the most common.

In some cases the police may want to carry out further investigations, such as searching a teenager's room, or collecting blood or urine samples, for which the law gives no actual authority. (Powers like those for testing suspected drunken drivers by means of the breathalyser or blood samples do not extend to drugs, or even to alcohol in non-drivers. Curiously enough, even a person suspected of being drunk in charge of a vehicle is not obliged to subject himself to a test, though the law provides penalties if he refuses to do so.)

Depending on the age of the suspect, either he or his parents could be asked for permission to take a blood or urine specimen. If this was refused, no penalties apply in a drugs case and samples could not be taken compulsorily. On the other hand, a magistrate's warrant (valid for a month) could be obtained for searching a house, entering by force if necessary. A solicitor's advice would almost always be valuable in deciding whether to give permission for samples of blood or urine to be taken. Agreement to a test which revealed no drugs would obviously be in the suspect's favour. But a few convictions for unauthorized possession have been based, in the absence of other evidence, on the presence of drugs in urine specimens. If agreement is given, it is vital that the test specimen should be divided, so that part can be analysed separately on behalf of the accused person.

A teenager may already have made a verbal or written statement before the parents arrive, but if not it would be advisable to consult a solicitor before making a statement which could well be used in court.

Once a suspect has been formally charged, he will usually be released on bail and required to attend court (or juvenile court) next morning. Before the hearing, all concerned should go very carefully into the details of the alleged offence with the solicitor. Unless the facts are crystal clear, he will almost certainly advise pleading 'not guilty'. At the hearing itself, a postponement (technically known as an 'adjournment') may be granted at the request of either the police or the defendant (in person, or through his solicitor if one has been instructed). An adjournment will almost invariably be granted if there has been insufficient time to prepare the case. Seven days from the date of being charged is usually accepted by the court as being the minimum reasonable period for preparation of the defence, particularly if witnesses are to be called. Serious offences involving large quantities of drugs are usually tried by a jury in a higher court, but the great majority of cases against young people for possession of small quantities of drugs are dealt with summarily in a magistrate's or juvenile court. Though the prosecution cannot always do so, an accused person always has the right to choose trial by jury even in a 'minor' drugs case.

The police have powers under both the above acts to 'seize, and detain for the purpose of proceedings, anything found in the course of a search which appears to the constable to be evidence of an offence'. Some convictions for unauthorized possession have been based on traces of heroin found in a syringe, or on small fragments of cannabis. After conviction, any articles which were the subject of an offence are forfeited.

Maximum penalties on summary conviction (lesser offences in a magistrate's court) are as follows:—
Under the Dangerous Drugs Act (heroin, cocaine, marihuana etc.)—£250 fine, 12 months imprisonment, or both.
Under the Drugs (Prevention of Misuse) Act (amphetamines, hallucinogens etc.)—£200 fine, six months imprisonment, or both.

Maximum penalties on conviction on indictment (more serious offences heard in a higher court):—
Under the Dangerous Drugs Act—£1,000 fine, 10 years imprisonment, or both.
Under the Drugs (Prevention of Misuse) Act—a fine of unlimited size, two years imprisonment, or both.

In practice, the actual sentences imposed on young first offenders found with a few amphetamine tablets or reefers range from conditional discharge to a period of probation or a small fine. (Conditional discharge means that nothing more is heard of the case, provided that the defendant is not convicted of a further offence.) Even repeated offences seldom attract anything like maximum penalties, which are reserved for pushers (pedlars) rather than drug-takers.

III   Addicts' slang

Acid: LSD
Acid-head: LSD-taker
Artillery: addict's syringe, etc.

Bag: U.S. term for dose of heroin
Bang: injection or its effect
Bennies: Benzedrine tablets (amphetamine)
Big D: LSD
Biz: injection equipment
Black bomber: Durophet (amphetamine)
Black and white (minstrel): Durophet (amphetamine)
Blocked: under influence of drug, usually amphetamine
Blow: to smoke cannabis
Blue acid: blue-coloured pills of LSD
Blues: Edrisal, Drinamyl or other blue amphetamine tablets

Boy: U.S. term for heroin

Brought down: depressed 'hangover' after-effect of
  drugs

Bullet: capsule

Buzz: effect of a drug

C: cocaine

Candy: barbiturates

Caps: capsules

Charge: marihuana

Charlie: cocaine

Chief: LSD

Coke: cocaine

Cokie: cocaine-taker

Cold turkey: untreated withdrawal of heroin

Come down: to stop taking drugs

Connection: U.S. term for drug pedlar, usually heroin

Cook up: to prepare an injection, usually of heroin

Cut: to adulterate drugs with sugar etc.

Dex: dexedrine tablets (amphetamine)

Dixies (Dexies): dexedrine tablets (amphetamine)

Dominoes: black and white capsules of Durophet
  (amphetamine)

Drying out: stopping or reducing dose of heroin

Dust: cocaine

Experience: LSD trip

Fix: injection, usually of heroin and/or cocaine

Flash: initial effect of stimulant, cocaine or amphetamine

199

French blue: Drinamyl or other blue amphetamine
  tablet

Gage: cannabis
Gear: addict's syringe, etc.
Goofballs: U.S. term for barbiturates
Grass: cannabis, usually marihuana
Green and black: Librium capsules (tranquillizer)
Gun: addict's syringe

H: heroin
H and C: heroin and cocaine
Habit: dependence on a drug
Happening: effect of marihuana or LSD, also group
  use
Harry: heroin
Hash: cannabis, usually resin
Hawk: LSD
Hay: cannabis, usually marihuana
High: effect of (stimulant) drugs
Hooked: addicted, usually to heroin
Horse: heroin

Ice-cream habit: occasional drug-taking
Instant Zen: LSD

Jack: heroin, particularly in tablet form
Joint: reefer (cannabis cigarette)
Jolly beans: amphetamine tablets
Joy pop: to inject heroin or morphine under skin
  before addiction develops
Junk: heroin (morphine, cocaine or other drugs)

Junkie: heroin addict

Kick: effect of stimulant drug, cocaine or amphetamine
Kick habit: to stop taking drugs

Locoweed: cannabis, usually marihuana

M: morphine
Mainline: to inject drugs directly into a vein (usually
heroin, morphine, cocaine or methyl amphetamine)
Meth: methedrine tablets or injection (methyl amphe-
tamine)
Minstrel: black and white Durophet capsules (amphe-
tamine)
Miss Emma: morphine

Needle: addict's syringe etc.
Nod: to doze off after dose of drugs (to be 'on the nod')

Pad: room, flat, etc.
Pillhead: tablet-taker, usually amphetamines
Pot: cannabis
Pot-head: cannabis smoker
Psychedelic experience: effect of LSD or other hallu-
cinogen
Purple heart: Drinamyl (old shape), sometimes used
for amphetamines in general
Pusher: drug pedlar

Reefer: marihuana cigarette
Resin: cannabis resin, hashish etc.

The Willing Victim

Rope: cannabis

Scrip (script): prescription for habit-forming drugs
Shit: heroin
Shoot up: to inject drugs, usually into a vein 'mainline'
Shot: injection of drugs
Sick: withdrawal symptoms, usually from heroin
Skin popping: injection under the skin, usually heroin
Sleepers: barbiturates
Snow: cocaine
Speedball: combined injection of heroin (or morphine)
    with cocaine (or methyl amphetamine)
Spike: addict's syringe, etc.
Stick: marihuana cigarette or 'reefer'
Sugar: LSD, not necessarily on sugar lump
Sweets: amphetamine (or other) coloured tablets

Tea: marihuana
Trip: effect of LSD or other hallucinogen
Turn on: to start another person on drugs
Turned on: to be under the influence of drugs

Weed: cannabis, usually marihuana
Works: addict's syringe, etc.

Zen: LSD

IV Trade names and brief descriptions of commonly used drugs, which could be abused

1. *Some stimulants etc., controlled by the Drugs (Prevention of Misuse) Act 1964*

Amphetamine: plain white tablets, roughly aspirin-sized.

Apisate: largish yellow tablet; W in shield on one side.

Dexamphetamine: plain tablets, white or yellow, sometimes with line on one side.

Dexedrine: flat yellow tablets with line on one side and SKF on other.

Dexedrine (long-acting): two sizes of capsules,

brown one end, transparent the other, containing orange and white granules—like 'hundreds and thousands'.

Dexten: large, flat yellow tablet with cross on one side, marked N and 'dexten' on the other.

Duromine: small size, capsule green one end, grey other, marked Riker: larger size, maroon and grey capsule marked Riker.

Durophet: small size, white capsule marked Riker: medium size, white and black capsule marked Riker: large size, black capsule marked Riker: 'black bombers'.

Euvitol: yellow tablets or green liquid.

Filon: orange-yellow sugar-coated tablet.

Lucophen SA: largish white tablets.

Mephine: ampoules of solution.

Mephentermine: plain tablets.

Methedrine: plain white tablets with line on one side, 'tabloid brand' on reverse.

Methylamphetamine: plain white tablets, or glass ampoules containing colourless solution.

Neo-endrine: nasal spray in plastic bottle.

Parnate: red sugar-coated tablets marked SKF.

Preludin: flat white tablet marked P on one side and line on other.

Preludin (long-acting): large yellow tablets with 'castle' design on one side.

Ritalin: white tablets marked CIBA on one side, line with two dots on other, also ampoules of solution.

Tenuate: plain white tablet, resembling large aspirin.

Tenuate Dospan (long-acting): white bolster-shaped tablet with line across middle.

Villescon: orange sugar-coated tablet marked with 'castle' design, or orange liquid.

2. *Some mixed stimulants and other drugs controlled by the Drugs (Prevention of Misuse) Act 1964*

Anxine: white sugar-coated tablets.

Appetrol: pink tablets.

Appetrol SR (long-acting): pink-topped capsules.

Barbidex: large, flat tablet, cross on one side, marked N and 'barbidex' on other.

Daprisal: yellow, pillow-shaped tablet marked SKF on one side.

Dexdale: green tablets, line one side, DPL on other.

Dexytal: bright pink capsules.

Drinamyl: pale mauve-blue tablets with line on one side; 'purple hearts'.

Drinamyl spansules (long-acting): capsules, green one end, transparent other, filled with green and white granules; two sizes.

Durophet M: small size, green and brown capsules: large size, red and brown capsules.

Edrisal: plain blue tablets marked SKF on one side.

Parstelin: green sugar-coated tablets marked SKF, also as a liquid.

Potensan: maroon sugar-coated tablet.

Potensan forte: gold-coated pill.

Steladex: capsule, transparent and yellow, filled with blue and white granules.

Stimplete: orange-coloured liquid.

3. *Some commonly used barbiturate preparations*

Amytal : small, plain white tablets.

Carbrital : white capsule with blue line around middle.

Nembutal : bright yellow capsules.

Phenobarbitone : small, plain white tablets.

Phenobarbitone (long-acting) : capsules, blue one end, transparent other, containing blue and white granules.

Seconal : orange-red capsules.

Sodium amytal : bright blue capsules.

Soneryl : pink tablets with line on one side.

Tuinal : capsules, orange-red one end, blue other.

4. *Some commonly used tranquillizers and non-barbiturate sleeping drugs*

Doriden : plain white tablet marked CIBA.

Equanil : tablets in two sizes—yellow and white.

Largactil : white, sugar-coated tablets, syrup or injection ampoules. (Used to terminate 'bad' LSD trips.)

Librium : small size, green and yellow capsules : large size, green and black capsules. (Also as glass ampoules containing powder.)

Mandrax : capsules : dark blue one end, light blue other, marked *Mx* RL, tablets : flat white, marked Mx on one side, and RL on other.

Miltown : large size, white tablets with line across : small size, white sugar-coated tablets.

Miltown S.R. (long-acting) : blue-topped capsules.

Mogadon : White tablet, 'Roche' on one side with semicircles, line on reverse.

Oblivon : capsules, or as blue liquid.

Names and Descriptions of Commonly Used Drugs

Oblivon C: oval, blue sugar-coated tablets.

Sparine: three strengths: yellow, orange and red sugar-coated tablets, also injection ampoules and syrup.

Stelazine: blue tablets, sugar-coated, marked SKF (two sizes); also in ampoules or in clear, greeny-yellow syrup.

Stelazine (long-acting form): capsules blue one end, yellow the other (three sizes).

Valium: white, yellow or blue tablets (three sizes), also as capsules, syrup and injection solution in ampoules.